"We may think we know all there is to know about international adoption—isn't it constantly in the news? Aren't celebrities doing it? A memoir like *from ashes to africa* reminds us of the uniqueness and poignancy of each family's journey, of the sorrow and longing that often precedes the discovery of a child, and of a joy sweeter and more miraculous for having been delayed."

-Melissa Fay Greene, author of *There Is
No Me Without You: An Ethiopian Woman's
Odyssey to Rescue her Country's Children*

"I strongly recommend this book to you. It will make you laugh and cry, but most important, once you put it down you will never be the same again."

-Tom Davis, author of *Red Letters:
Living a Faith that Bleeds*

"If you ever find yourself asking the question, 'Where are the God stories today of personal transformation?' then look no further! This book will provide a compelling answer to that question. With humor, transparency, and poignancy, Josh and Amy share their life-changing journey in such a way that will not leave the reader unchanged."

-Dave and Jan Dravecky, co-authors
of *When You Can't Come Back*

"This book offers the reader hope, encouragement, laughter, and optimism. You will empathize with Josh and Amy as they openly write about issues they had to face when it came to their marriage, their struggle with infertility, and ultimately the decision to adopt their son from Ethiopia. No matter what your current situation might be, whether you are just looking to be encouraged, are going through infertility, or are already in the midst of your adoption journey, this is a must read. If adopting couples would take to heart some of the nuggets in this book, I believe their whole adoption experience would be enhanced."

-J. Scott Brown, Executive Vice President,
The Gladney Center for Adoption

"Josh and Amy tell a lovely story of how they saved their lives by giving them away. In a world given to grasping and getting, they found their eyes opened to Jesus' image in
'the least, the last, and the lost.' Josh and Amy's difficult journey of infertility led not to the expected ashes of disappointment and despair. Instead it took a path to Africa and to adoption—an alternative journey, which led unexpectedly to 'beautiful headdresses, oils of gladness, and garments of praise (Isaiah 61:3).' In their journey, they showed us how to escape the pull of selfishness by 'bringing good news to the poor and binding up the brokenhearted.' In healing others, we heal ourselves. In blessing others, we find ourselves blessed."

-Dr. Jay Lorenzon, Founder of Families for Africa

"This book is an amazingly heartfelt, pure, really well-written story of world-changing redemption."

-Lance Humphreys, Senior Pastor, Bridgeway Church

"Books are difficult to write and even more difficult to write with a spouse. Josh and Amy don't hold back as they offer us their story from unfaith to faith, from despair to hope, from strife to partnership, from an empty home to parenting a child, from Oklahoma City to Addis Ababa. They model the kind of honesty that helps us remember why we need a saving Lord. Reading this book will not allow any couple to go back to business as usual."

-Josh Banner, Minister of Arts and Music, Hope College

"How does one recapture the dream of marriage and family when hope is dead? This book bleeds hard won truth from life experiences. As counselors who saw the beginning of this couple's doomed relationship, we can tell you that you're reading a remarkable story. The journey *from ashes to africa* will thrill you with the goodness of God and challenge you with the insightful story of those who persevered and learned to love God and each other in a new way."

-Scott and Ann Manley, Director of
Cornerstone Network Ministries

"Let's be honest: it's easy not to think about miserable places or situations if we don't want to—or, when we do, to send a little chunk of money. Josh and Amy Bottomly write about the outrageous decision to welcome an Ethiopian child into their lives—a decision that will never allow them to be arm-chair activists again. Of course it wasn't easy; they write with sincerity and thoughtfulness about their struggle with infertility and, in that struggle, discover another option. They offer therein a compelling and acute sense that the typical American model for family is often too thin, too sugary—like the soda pop we down in aluminum cans. You'll not soon forget the Bottomlys' powerful journey to live beyond that model and how that transformation connects them—and me, and you, and all of us—to a global community of humans in need: orphans—all 143 million of them."

-Dr. Susanna Childress, poet, Jagged with Love

from ashes to africa

JOSH AND AMY BOTTOMLY

from ashes to africa

a memoir

TATE PUBLISHING & *Enterprises*

Published by Tate Publishing & Enterprises, LLC
127 E. Trade Center Terrace | Mustang, Oklahoma 73064 USA
1.888.361.9473 | www.tatepublishing.com

Tate Publishing is committed to excellence in the publishing industry. The company reflects the philosophy established by the founders, based on Psalm 68:11,
"The Lord gave the word and great was the company of those who published it."

Book design copyright © 2008 by Tate Publishing, LLC. All rights reserved.
Cover design by Stefanie Rooney
Interior design by Nathan Harmony

Published in the United States of America

ISBN: 978–1-60604–598–5
1. Family & Relationships: Adoption
2. Biography & Autobiography: Personal Memoirs
08.12.01

Dedication

To Hermela
For your courage, love, and sacrifice

Acknowledgments

We have a kaleidoscope of people to thank for helping us along the way on our adoption journey. We'd like to begin by thanking Scott and Ann Manley. We're proud to be considered your "trophy couple"! We want to thank Jamie and Gretchen Miller. You planted the seed in us to write this book. There would be no tree without you. We'd also like to express gratitude to Whitney Knowles for her energetic, meticulous, and thoughtful editing. Your feedback could not have been more helpful in polishing our prose. Additionally, we'd like to thank Jaime McNutt Bode, our Tate editor. We appreciate your hawk's eye for details. Moreover, we'd like to thank those of you who contributed financially to our adoption costs. This list includes Glen and Joyce DeMaranville (Amy's parents), Roc and Bev Bottomly (Josh's parents), Bow and Megan Bottomly (Silas's godparents), Brandon and Sherry Sage (close friends), and Tracy Hanson (Junkposse Jewelry Owner). We particularly want to thank Mark Aduddell, pastor of Expression Church, for helping us with the Jubilee transaction. Finally, we have to give a warm round of applause to the Gladney staff for our entire adoption experience. It was "frictionless" from start to finish. Specifically, we are grateful for the courageous vision of Scott Brown, the infectious enthusiasm of Mary Thottukadavil, the amazing professionalism of Belay Tafesse, the mission-guided hearts of Ryan and Abby Brown, and the tender nurture of Silas's caretaker.

Table of Contents

Foreword

In 1989, my wife, Emily, and I adopted our daughter, Anya, from Russia.

My eyes were suddenly awakened to a world made up of 144 million orphans, and I was forced into a crossroad: I could escape back into my cozy lifestyle or engage the world Anya and others like her came from. Standing in Anya's dirty, dark orphanage, that decision became crystal clear. Two girls bolted out of the crowd of children, hugged my legs for dear life, and said to me, "Papa, papa." How could I leave them there and walk away?

My choice, along with my wife's, led me to Children's Hope Chest, an organization devoted to creating a world where every orphan knows God's love, experiences family, and acquires the skills necessary for independent life. Serving as Hope Chest's president, I helped to launch orphan programs in impoverished parts of the world in Russia and Africa. My firsthand experiences inspired me to write *Fields of the Fatherless*, a book meant to remind Christians that the

God of Israel, incarnated in Jesus, calls us to care for the "least of these," specifically the widow and orphan.

In 2007, I wrote a sequel entitled *Red Letters: Living a Faith that Bleeds*, a book meant to call the church to become incarnational agents of Christ's compassion and bring justice to the marginalized and disenfranchised. In other words, it was a call to action.

A couple responding to that call is Josh and Amy Bottomly. I am happy to call them friends. They are two followers of Jesus who are serious about the heart of God and are committed to helping needy orphans in our world. Through their adoption of Silas from Ethiopia, Josh and Amy had their Damascus road experience and could no longer go back to life as normal. Ironically, it was through Josh and Amy's personal suffering that God led them into the society of the suffering, and more specifically, into a place where millions of orphans daily lack food, shelter, education, medical care, clean water, and most importantly, love and nurture. This journey taught Josh and Amy about God's healing and wholeness, and they have found their calling and common mission.

Today Josh and Amy have locked arms with Children's Hope Chest, along with The Red Letters Campaign, to launch a new orphan care program in Ethiopia some time in the summer of 2009.

I strongly recommend this book to you. It will make you laugh and cry, but most important, once you put it down you will never be the same again.

Fighting for the Fatherless,
Tom Davis

Introduction

"We read to know we are not alone." *Shadowlands*[i]

Josh

On the first day of graduate school, Dr. Garrison strolled into class with his dignified gait, clad in his rumpled blazer with the brown elbow patches. His leather binder was stuffed with lecture notes, and his bow tie was crooked underneath his flabby chin. Notably, Dr. Garrison's eyes and nose reminded me of a tortoise, like the ones photographed in *National Geographic* that paddle off the shores of the Galapagos Islands.

As Dr. Garrison opened to his notes and leaned his arms on the podium, I fidgeted in my desk as though Oklahoma fire ants were skittering through my boxer shorts. "Esteemed future colleagues," the professor warbled in a throaty way, "will one of you please tell me why God created man? "I didn't utter a peep. Neither did any of my classmates. We knew of Dr. Garrison's notorious reputation for smashing student's responses like cheap porcelain. Feeling our unease, Dr. Garrison grinned and beckoned us forward with his index finger; we scooted up to the edge of our chairs to listen. "God," Dr. Garrison whispered before pausing for a moment to let the word gather firmly in the air. "*God created man because he loves stories.*"

It's true, I think, that God loves stories because he is the inventor of them, and more than anything, he delights in using "prop actors" to play lead roles in one of his epic screenplays.

By my own admission, I have often felt like Neo in *The Matrix*, reticent and lacking aplomb, convinced that God must have the wrong protagonist in mind. I have nothing titanic to offer to the part. I am a simple English teacher and basketball coach (currently with an inauspicious record of 7–13). In addition, neither Amy nor I hold influential positions in our church, community, or jobs, and truthfully, we are okay with that. We tend to eschew the spotlight. Amy prefers a chameleon-like existence, where she can blend into the wallpaper. I tend to favor a monastic-like existence, where I can live unmolested in my cave of books. What Amy and I, though, have witnessed firsthand demands a whole-hearted response. We have discovered a world within our world made up over 144,000 million orphans, 4.4 million in Ethiopia alone. As a result, Amy and I can't go back to life as normal. We feel summoned to a *lifestyle of involvement* with the "least of these."

Amy and I obviously don't have much to contribute. We're not billionaires like Bill and Melinda Gates. We're not rock stars like Bono. We're not movie stars like Brad and Angelina. Instead, Amy and I are like two bumbling hobbits. We know we can't save Middle-Earth, but we also know we can't live comfortably in the Shire. If, though, Amy and I have come to believe anything, it is that there is one who can take two people's paltry lives of "five loaves and two fish" and make it grow, expand, and multiply into a sumptuous feast. Believing this, Amy and I celebrate the way God longs to use ordinary people to accomplish his extraordinary purposes in places like Ethiopia.

T.S. Eliot once wrote:

> *These are only hints and guesses,*
> *Hints followed by guesses; and the rest*
> *Is prayer, observance, discipline, thought and action.*[2]

Our story mirrors Eliot's understanding of spirituality and faith. Through our entire journey, Amy and I have wobbled along on tentative legs as we have tried to wisely guess and prayerfully discern the voice that more often than not speaks to us in whispers and in shadows.

Specifically, this is the story of *ashes*. For us, our ashes correspond to our battles with barrenness. Studies show that one-third of the time, infertility involves the female. One-third of the time, it involves the male. Another one-third involves mystery. Three-thirds of the time, though, infertility involves deep heartache and pain. Amy and I know this firsthand.

This is also the story of *Africa*. For us, our story involves falling in love with and feeling God's heart for a continent and people, where beauty and tragedy, wealth and poverty, and humanity and sub-humanity coexist in a jagged tension. Stepping into this world of interlocking realities felt like a baptism of sorts, whereupon returning to Oklahoma, we have been challenged and inspired to rethink and redo everything from our relationship with God, to church and community, to our understanding of missions and God's future dreams for the earth.

Finally, this is the story of *adoption*. For us, it is simply the story of meeting a baby boy named Tesfamariam, and our lives not being the same since.

Ashes

"Writing is really quite simple; all you have to do is
sit down at your typewriter and open a vein."
Frederick Buechner, *The Clown in the Belfry*[3]

Starting a Family

Josh

Amy and I disagree over the time and place when we first broached the topic of children.

My version goes like this.

Amy and I were still practically newlyweds, only married nine months. We were in Florida on vacation with my family. One evening Amy and I took a walk on the beach. That particular dusky night, the sunset looked like a scarlet ribbon holding the sky and ocean together. With sugary sand between our toes and the smell of seaweed and the briny surf in our noses, we began to let the sound of the crashing waves lull us into deep reveries. Suddenly, I could see a boy in my mind's eye. He was the spitting image of me: a mop of red curls and a face full of freckles, a natural lefty for a baseball pitcher. At the same time, Amy nurtured dreams of a little girl with almond-shaped eyes and auburn locks, her Easter dress flapping in the warm spring breeze as she skipped toward a chocolate egg hidden behind the hawthorn bushes.

Amy

All I recall about the Bottomly family vacation to Florida was that I felt like I was at a breaking point.

The first nine months of our marriage had been anything but a honeymoon. Josh and I had spent most of our first year fighting like Britney Spears and Kevin Federline, our veins popping out and our esophagi burning with vitriolic acids.

Josh and I had been told by other married couples that the honeymoon might be all "sex and chocolate chip pancakes," but marriage was a different dish altogether. The common refrain I had heard from my friends was, "Slow down! You barely know each other." They had a compelling point. I had met Josh on a blind date through a mutual friend in September of 2000. A month later, when Josh asked me to move down from Iowa to Oklahoma, his intentions were crystal clear: he wanted to pursue my hand in marriage. I didn't blink an eye when I said yes. Two weeks later Josh slipped a diamond ring on my finger, and five months later, as the last winter storm blanketed the Iowa cornfields, I said "I do" to Josh before a congregation holding their fingers crossed behind their backs.

Looking back, I'm not sure if a wrecking ball would have been able to smash through my walls of rationalization for marrying Josh so quickly. Honestly, what girl doesn't dream of a torrid romance and having a *Jerry Maguire* moment where the guy says, "You complete me," and in a crying quiver she responds, "You had me at hello."

Josh did have me at "hello." But soon after I said "I do," he almost lost me.

Invisible Monsters

Josh

I'll admit that my somewhat quixotic memory tends to erase the bad memories and laminate the good ones. For example, I still like to relive the euphoria of winning the basketball state championship my junior year in high school and forget the agony of losing it my senior year.

Amy's right, though. Our first year of marriage was like an episode of *Lost*. Saying "I do" was the equivalent of crashing a plane on a deserted island. Our vows meant we were stuck on the island, and there was no getting off. We had to find a way not only to survive on the island but to combat and defeat the invisible, carnivorous Thing.

For us, the Thing was a three-headed monster.

The Monster of Disillusionment. It wasn't very long before Amy and I felt disappointed in each other. We had failed to live up to each other's high expectations. For me, it started on our wedding night. I was a virgin. The way I pictured it, our first night would resemble Jack and Rose in the *Titanic*, our bodies melting into each other, releasing steam, moisture, and heat into the earth's atmosphere.

Instead our first night was filled with fog and rain and ice. Amy bawled through it like she had just watched the end of *Titanic*. She was inconsolable. I vividly recall retreating to the bathroom in our hotel. Grabbing the sides of my head, I thought, *It is only the first night, and already I am unable to excite my wife. What's wrong with me? Is it my breath? My aftershave? My body? Has Amy suddenly discovered that I don't have chiseled abs?* I felt a sudden blast of anger, panic, and resentment. It caused me to believe that our marriage was already set on a course doomed like the Titanic!

For Amy, her disappointment began with our honeymoon. She had expected an all-inclusive hotel, outfitted with room service, chatoyant pools, spa treatments, cascading waterfalls, beachside beds, and strawberry daiquiris. Instead she got a pink shanty, Wal-Mart food, and rainy weather that forced us to remain stuck inside playing endless hands of Hearts and Spades. One night I heard Amy crying in the bathroom. She had just uncovered a gecko slithering through our cabin-yellow colored blankets.

Upon returning from our honeymoon, the crack in our marital illusions quickly spider webbed out. I had envisioned lazy Sunday afternoons in our bedroom, our flesh intertwined underneath satin sheets, and our mouths full of amorous laughter. Instead I spent more time curled up at the opposite end of the bed. I would quietly fume and roil. My thoughts would coil inward like a conch shell. *I know I'm no Matthew*

McConaughey, but is my figure that repulsive to Amy? And what does Amy have against going over to my parents' house on Sunday for family night? Doesn't she know it's a Bottomly tradition? And how come Amy gets to manage the monthly budget? If Amy thinks she can reduce my golf and book allowance and increase her designer jean and pedicure funds, well, she's got another thing coming!

The Monster of Twenty-Something Pressures. It started with Amy moving her whole life from Iowa to Oklahoma City. For the first year, she struggled miserably to make friends, find a job, and deal with the family distance. Equally stressful was the fact that I was making only $19,500 as a Christian schoolteacher, with zero medical benefits. We could barely afford rent, let alone furniture. It didn't help when Amy ran up a cell phone bill for $748.00 before we got married. Soon collection agencies threatened to garner our wages. Amy had to call her father for a small loan. I was too embarrassed to ask her father, Glen. I felt like it was already a sign that I couldn't hack it as the provider. This feeling was only exacerbated at the end of the month. As Amy held a stack of bills like a poker hand, I knew I couldn't bluff my way out. I had been called, exposed, revealed for the inept husband that I was. I felt the waters rising over my head in terms of real "adult responsibilities." Before Amy and I knew it, the combination of debt, distance, and a dead-end job had drowned us in stress and anxiety.

The Monster of Human Sinfulness. One day I got snoopy and leafed through Amy's journal. It was a weasel-like thing to do. What I read shocked me. Her prose was holes in walls made by irascible fists that included words and phrases like "arrogant," "condescending," "prone to lies," and a "sad and pathetic person." When I talked specifically about God and the Bible, I made Amy feel like her theology was too basic, her prayers too simplistic, and her worldview too one-dimensional. I can't blame Amy for her naked honesty. My journal wasn't much different. Many entries read like Hamlet's soliloquies, full of hyperbolic ranting and clandestine brooding over Amy's refusal to embrace my friends, church, and family. It wasn't like I was looking for Amy to become a fawning Stepford wife. I just didn't want to stay married to a frothing Doberman pinscher.

I knew that if we didn't get help ASAP, Amy and I would inevitably be swallowed into the belly of the beast.

Manleys to the Rescue

Amy

Josh and I heard about an older couple named Scott and Ann Manley. Young couples in the church community knew them for their aged wisdom and honest counsel. What I liked most was that neither of them knew Josh nor me. They could be an impartial and objective voice.

When Josh and I first met with Scott and Ann, we took turns telling our side of things. Scott and Ann listened sympathetically to both of us. While Josh shared his side of things with thinly veiled anger, I just let it all hang out, spilling my pent-up frustration through tears and sobs. By the time I finished talking, there were enough balled-up Kleenex at my feet to roll around in and make a snow angel.

After we finished, Ann was the first to speak. She generally was. Her words were sharp and penetrating, like ammunition capable of piercing bulletproof metal. She was hardest on Josh. Ann took aim at Josh for not sticking up for me when one of Josh's friends or family members complained about me. "If an unspoken line is drawn in the sand," Ann explained, her beady eyes boring a hole into Josh like a drill sergeant on the first day of boot camp, "you'd better make sure everyone knows whose side you are on, and that's Amy's." Josh listened at erect attention with unflinching eyes, absorbing Ann's criticism like a cadet in training.

That's not to say I didn't occasionally get dragged out in front of the firing squad. I distinctly recall Ann telling me that Josh and I were mutually responsible and accountable to God for creating an environment in which the other could thrive spiritually. Ann knew I wasn't doing my part. More importantly, I knew it. I had watched Josh's passion for the Lord grow wan and dim. Much of what had imbued his spirit with life had faded away.

When Ann finished admonishing both of us, Scott would follow up with a more tender word. For me, Scott was a reservoir of gentleness. He had "Jesus eyes"—his gaze brought me warmth and peace. Every time I fell apart, he was the first to offer a tissue or a hug. I loved him instantly like my own father. I remember distinctly how at the end of the first session, Scott looked at both of us and quietly said, "It sounds to me like you two have *clashing dreams*." It was an epiphany that resonated truth. Scott saw the withering tree that was our marriage and immediately dug below the soil to expose the broken roots. Ann followed up with a painful prescription for a restorative path, "Before you seriously start thinking about having children, I think you should focus on laying a strong foundation for your family. This may take longer than you hoped."

I really didn't want to hear that, but I agreed. Rather than healing our wounds, children would probably hemorrhage them.

We met regularly with the Manleys for almost a year, and often on unscheduled occasions. The Manleys became our emergency paramedics. One time, after Josh and I had a "knockdown drag-out fight" (as Ann put it), I left our apartment and somehow ended up outside the Manleys' house. Emotionally disheveled and in need of solace, I called them from my cell phone. Scott answered and told me to come over. I instructed him to look out his window. I waved.

Many things happened during our time with the Manleys. We faced our disillusionment and learned how to give each other permission to just be ourselves. For example, I validated Josh's monkish side, letting him more regularly retreat into his cave (guest room), releasing him to connect with God in the ways that animated his soul. On the flip side, I saw Josh shift from merely tolerating my "pop-culture side" to embracing it, like grabbing Chili's take out for dinner and joining me in front of the television to cheer on my favorite *American Idol* contestant.

In addition, we overcame some of our early marriage pressures. Josh got a better paying job, and I finally got a job. We bought a house. Monthly housing payments went up, but phone bills filled with long-distance distress calls went down. We made new friends. We became more involved in our church.

Finally, we dealt with our sin. As God exposed the junk in our hearts (often through the utterances of Scott or Ann), we repented and sought the grace to change. Marriage, as I soon discovered, was much easier when both people were humbly moving toward God.

Years later Scott and Ann admitted that after our first meeting, they thought our marriage was beyond repair. They seriously considered taking us down to the courthouse to get an annulment. They had never solicited this kind of "emergency counsel" to a couple before. But we weren't like any other couple they had encountered.

I agree with Josh now that if we had not sprinted to the altar in only six months time but rather dated for a long stretch, we most likely wouldn't have gotten married. I laugh now because I see how our first year was like being players on the reality game show *Survivor*, but in God's version of the show, the goal was not to connive, manipulate, and backstab the other to win the million bucks. Instead the goal was to cling to, fight for, and lean on each other like we had never done before with anyone.

In hindsight, I realize that God used the Manleys not only to lay a more solid foundation for our family but also to lay the groundwork for the difficult days ahead when we started trying to have a bigger family, one that included a child.

Becoming Dad

Josh

Three years later, with a firm foundation beneath us, Amy and I decided to start trying for kids. Our close friends, Brandon and Sherry Sage, had just gotten pregnant. We had always talked with them about having children at the same time. Brandon and I dreamed of our sons growing up to be star athletes together, one as the quarterback, the other as the wide receiver, like Tom Brady and Randy Moss.

I assumed we would have no problem starting a family. Virility ran through my bloodline like the Mississippi River through the Midwest. I was almost a honeymoon baby. As a result, I swelled with all the fortissimo of Babe Ruth, pointing to right field, fully confident that with one swing of the bat—boom! Crack! Zoom! Home Run!

During those days of trying, I could barely hold a thought in my head about becoming a father. Growing up like any firstborn son, I viewed my dad as a hero; he towered over my imagination. As a boy, I remember standing under our fireplace, staring up within the silver glow of my dad's sword. It was the centerpiece of the living room, our family's unspoken symbol. It wasn't just any sword, though; it was Dad's graduation sword, the one he received when he graduated from the Air Force Academy. As I scanned my eyes from the chromatic shaft across the steely blade, I would imagine Dad in the moonlight, no longer a pastor (his profession at the time) but transformed into a King Arthur, or a Samurai warrior, or better yet, turned into Leo, my favorite Teenage Mutant Ninja Turtle, battling his arch nemesis, Splinter.

It's no coincidence, then, that my childhood memories were thick with father-son moments. Most of them involved sports, either with Dad as my coach or my number one fan. To this day, I still can't get the pulpy taste out of my mouth from Saturday mornings playing soccer and eating orange slices after the game with Dad, usually to celebrate our victory over the Green Wave. I also can't get the smell of Dad's fleece out of my nose, the one that smelled of chimney smoke and Colorado pine, the fleece that Dad let me wipe my mucus-laden tears on after the homecoming game my senior year when I played my worst game, clanking all my shots in front of a jam-packed field house with college scouts looking on in the stands.

I thought of all the special moments I had shared with my family, especially my three siblings. I thought of the times when my brothers and I converted the living room couches into a wrestling ring, using the armchairs as turn-buckles, often standing on them only to fling ourselves down like Hulk Hogan on Andre the Giant. I thought of how in September our backyard converted into a football field, where we would pretend to play for the Dallas Cowboys, running button hooks around the peach tree, catching passes, and celebrating pretend touchdowns by spiking the pigskin in mom's tomato and cucumber garden. I thought of our family vacations, my favorites involving ski trips to Crested Butte and all six of us blazing down Paradise Bowl, jumping over moguls, and howling with laughter every time we'd come to a skidding halt, spraying white powder into the other's face.

No doubt then, as Amy took that first pregnancy test, I could barely suppress my excitement to become a dad and start a new chapter in the Bottomly family saga.

Becoming Mom

Amy

One of the initial things that attracted me to Josh was his love for his family. On our first date, while we shared bagels and coffee early one Saturday morning, Josh confessed how he hoped to have four children of his own. I only desired two kids, just like my family. Regardless of numbers, I found common ground to share with Josh in our desire for children.

Like Josh, I have wonderful memories with my dad. By his own admission, my dad always had a soft place in his heart for little girls in pigtails. To him, I was the quintessential manifestation of such cuteness. From as early as I can remember, Dad and I loved to sing together as we traveled somewhere in his old beat-up truck. For Dad, the oldies were the goodies. As we would drive down the road, my father and I would sway our heads to the melody, sometimes touching our foreheads like we were singing into the same microphone, every once-in-a-while hitting a note just perfectly, my alto harmonizing with his baritone. To this day, Dad and I love to break out spontaneously in a duet, singing favorites like Dee Clark's "Raindrops":

> So it must be rai-aindrops, so many raindrops
> It feels like raindrops
> Falling from my ey-eyes
> Falling from my eyes.

Oddly, Dad and I couldn't memorize a Bible verse to save our lives, but we could break into song at any stanza or chorus line and sing along verbatim. It was our special gift.

I could laminate many of my family memories in shimmering gold. I fondly remember my dad coming home smelling of sweat and pipe grease, and while he took a shower down in the basement, my mom would sit on the stool next to the shower curtain, where she would rehash her day while Dad scrubbed his body into a soapy lather. There was always something reassuring for me every time I heard the hiss of water moving through the floor pipes, causing the whole house to creak, gurgle, and groan.

My brother, Brian, and I were separated by seven years, so our relationship was somewhat strained by age. Nevertheless, we pinched and tussled our way through many marvelous years. For some reason, Brian's brotherly love language with me either involved pinning me down on all fours and then tickling my sides until I almost peed, or wrestling me into a headlock and giving me a "noogie" with his knuckle nubs until my cranium throbbed with ice-pick pain.

Outside of the home, Brian played the role of the Christian school kid rebel. I still recall driving to Grandview Park Baptist School every morning in his gray Monte Carlo, Brian always smelling of leather and cologne and trouble, and jamming out to Billy Idol or Van Halen on his cassette player. Being the good Christian girl that I was, I would regularly tattle on my brother to Mom for listening to "devil music." Later Brian would hunt me down and sock me in the arm, leaving a red mark on my bicep the size of a tennis ball.

As my mother's only daughter, she was a constant presence in my life, cheering me on at volleyball games, sitting front row at my musicals, helping me with my homework, and shopping with me for bargains at the mall. To this day, I still recall, as a little girl, changing into my dad's oversized white t-shirts and crawling in under my bed covers. Mom would turn out the light and sit next to my head, gently brushing my bangs away from my face while she prayed with me. Every night we asked God for the salvation of her family, along with my protection from Pike, the family monster that lived in our basement.

As a third grader, I still remember the mornings I'd grab for the handle of my lunch pail and thermos and feel its feathery lightness in my grip, instantly decoding what it meant— Mom was bringing me Taco John's for a lunch date!

In junior high, I loved hosting summertime sleepovers with my girlfriends. At night my mom would invent the most creative games to entertain us. One game I fondly remember involved Mom filling up two punch bowls with orange soda pop and then having us compete against each other to see who could suck down the soda the fastest through a straw.

The team that won tended to gloat by sticking their orange colored tongues out at the loser.

The more Josh and I talked about becoming parents and making our own family memories, the more anxious I became to rip open the box and whip out the pee stick to take that first pregnancy test.

Frustrating Days

Josh

The first pregnancy test was negative. We weren't discouraged, though. We quickly concluded that the Sages were the anomaly. For the average couple, it took a bit longer to conceive. The next month we tried again and got another negative sign. That time, the feelings of failure felt a little more pronounced. The next month we thought we had nailed it for sure. We did everything the books and experts had told us to do. We charted the cycle, we monitored the body's base temperatures, and we inspected the cervical mucus level (well, Amy did that). We felt like we had perfectly timed sex. And yet, three days later Amy started her menstrual cycle again.

Amy and I kept charting and trying, just as our doctor had ordered. One month Amy called me at work and in breathy excitement told me she thought for sure she was pregnant. She was three days late. She asked if I would pick up a pregnancy test, but I had already hung up on her mid-request. I was racing to the nearest Target, buying three different pregnancy tests, zooming home, and passing them on to Amy at the bathroom door. Outside the door, I chewed on my fingernails, pacing back and forth, trying not to itemize the sports paraphernalia I would buy for our future son or daughter's room. My train of thought was rudely interrupted by the sound of a loud flush and a shrieking expletive. Putting my ear up to the slit of the door, I could hear Amy trying to stifle a sob. I asked if she was okay; she told me to go away. She wanted to be left alone.

As I left our room and passed by our middle bedroom, I couldn't help but peek inside. Amy and I had planned to convert it into the baby's room, shading the walls petal pink or sky blue. For now though, the room was empty, smelling of dust, and covered in deep afternoon shadows. I quickly closed the door to that room as I tried to push away the dark thoughts that rumbled and intensified in my mind like Oklahoma wall clouds.

Amy

Living through the ups and downs of a monthly cycle felt like riding an endless roller coaster. At the start of every month, particularly during the "trying days," I always felt a surge of renewed hope. The middle part of the month wasn't bad either, as I anticipated test day. At times I felt like I was a little girl again, the December snow blanketing the earth and twinkling lights adorning the rooftops, while I waited anxiously under my covers until six AM rolled around—the hour my parents permitted me to rush out to discover what Santa left me under the Christmas tree. The end of the month, however, always left me feeling like the Grinch. Many nights I would stain my pillow with tears.

Before I knew it, a year had gone by. There were months toward the end of that year that we didn't try. The pressure had ballooned inside both of us, and the harder we tried, the more deflated we felt afterward. All the while, many girlfriends got pregnant. I remember Josh's sister calling me with her good news; I was barely able to keep from hanging up. It wasn't long before shower invitations began to arrive in the mail, and I'd feel my lip quivering just seeing the cream-colored cards. I'd tell friends I couldn't go, making up excuses for why, fearful I would be unable to mask my green-eyed jealousy.

Over time, a dark pall cast itself across my life. Everything fell inside its looming shadow. Friendships got harder. I can still remember going to lunch, my girlfriends talking about maternity clothes and foods they were craving, and I would just sit there and listen as I stared into my Caesar salad, feeling totally alienated from the conversation, realizing that a new club was forming of which I wasn't a part.

Sex got heavier. It became textbook-like and purely mechanical. I felt like suddenly we were the model couple in a book entitled *A Puritan Guide to Procreation*. Even church became unbearable. Because our church was full of young people, it wasn't long before it turned into a warren hopping with baby rabbits. They were everywhere, crawling and cooing around us, all dressed up in the cutest Baby Gap outfits. Vividly still, I can recall worship services where our friends would be clapping their hands, their eyes closed shut with sheer joy, their faces animated, their hearts full of praise, and I would just sit there empty, feeling blank, staring out through blurry eyes, my heart full of lead.

It wasn't long before Josh and I almost stopped everything. Friends. Sex. Church. We were tired of feeling a deep sense that we were missing out on everything that everybody else wasn't.

The Dreaded "I" Word

Josh

Amy read online that after a year of trying, doctors classify a couple as infertile. Trying to stay optimistic, I suggested that we just had a run of bad luck. It was like a hitter starting a season batting zero for twelve. All it took was one pitch, one clean swing, and one crack of the bat.

Secretly, though, both of us couldn't silence the voices in the back of our heads that fomented our worst fears. Finally, Amy asked me point blank: "Why don't you just get a sperm test?" Immediately, I cringed. The thought of a sterile room and a plastic cup and the awkwardness of knowing that the nurses and doctors knew what I was doing in the room next door…A shudder passed through my body. "Listen, babe,

Brandon took a sperm test just to 'dot the i's and cross the t's,'" Amy said, trying to coax me into calling the doctor." And if you want, I will come with you." I told Amy that would not be necessary.

A week later, I walked out of the doctor's office feeling confident that the results would put to bed any possibility that the problems were on my end. The next day the doctor's office called with the results.

At the time of the call, I was parked at Barnes and Noble, eager to make a mad dash through the freezing November rain to grab a cup of coffee. As sleet pelted the windshield, I cupped my ear around my cell phone to hear the nurse's words. "Your test shows—"

"You're going to have to speak louder. I can't hear with all the ice and sleet."

This time the nurse's voice crackled with clarity through the speaker. "Your test shows that you are infertile!"

I furled my eyebrows quizzically. I thought that for sure I must have picked up some white noise from the thump and pelt of the ice. "Come again?"

The nurse almost shouted this time. "*You are* going to need to see an infertility specialist. That's all I can tell you at this time." The nurse quickly hung up the phone before I could ask any questions. I don't remember much after that except the gelid feel of the steering wheel vinyl against my tear-soaked face.

After I gathered myself together in the car, I called my mom. I was too embarrassed to call Amy. The thought of telling her was too much. Little did I know that the nurse had already called Amy and informed her of my test results.

Amy had asked the nurse to call me. The thought of telling me was too much for Amy.

When I got Mom on the phone, I could barely get the lodged words out of my throat. There was a long silence on the other end of the line. "Infertile," she said, sounding like she had just choked on a throat lozenge. "Well, that can't be. There isn't infertility on either side of the family." I pressed the cell phone against my forehead. "Well, we'll be praying for you, and I'll have Dad call you later." The last person I wanted to talk to was my dad.

For the next fourteen days, there were moments where the mere thought of the "I" word made me feel like the sun was about to explode, sending my whole universe into chaos. For years, I had struggled internally with my sense of manhood. Like some men, I had successfully masked my insecurities, often behind jock talk and one-liners from movies like *The Godfather*, such as "I'll make him an offer he can't refuse." Behind my thin façade though, I felt a nagging fear that I was not a "real man." I taught English. I coached girls' basketball. I wasn't an IBF fan. I didn't own Apple stock. I didn't have an "expense account." When my guy friends would start talking business and punctuate the conversation with terms like "premiums," "market shares," and "NASDAQ index range," I'd space out and think, *If only we could talk about Jane Austen's* Pride and Prejudice *or John Steinbeck's* East of Eden.

Now my deepest anxiety was that over time, the "man" part of me would slowly disappear, and all that would remain was the "I" part.

"I," as in:

Infertile.

Incapable.

Inept.

Insecure.

Impotent.

As word leaked out that we had received some "bad news" on "some fertility tests," everyone I saw told me they were praying for us and our "unfortunate situation." Family. Friends. Pastors. They all reached out as best they could. But mostly I just wanted them to leave me alone. No shoulder hugs and head tilt expressions of sympathy. No Bible verses. No Christian bumper sticker quotes. Nothing.

From Failure to Failure

Amy

Josh and I were given the name of the best infertility doctor in Oklahoma City. The doctor had a billboard we had seen on the highway that celebrated 10,000 successful pregnancies. We hoped to be 10,001.

As we sat in his office with guarded optimism, the doctor hurled through the door, still dressed in his scrubs from an earlier surgery. Sitting down and quickly flipping through our file, he looked up and exclaimed matter-of-factly, "Josh, you're fine. The nurse misread your chart. You're loaded with good sperm. So there is that."

So *there* is *that*.

I looked over at Josh in a total daze and then asked the

doctor if I had misinterpreted his words. I hadn't. As Josh clapped his hands in celebration, I felt like tearing the handle off my chair. Not only did I want to sue the nurse and doctor for Josh's botched diagnosis, but I wanted to rip the doctor's smug smile right off his face. If Josh wasn't the problem, that meant I was. For two weeks I had been consoling Josh, telling him how much I loved and respected him as a man, and that if we never were able to have children, my feelings for him would never change.

Now I wondered if Josh would feel the same way about me.

The doctor quickly pulled me out of my downward spiral. He explained to me that he would start me off with blood work and follow it up in a couple weeks with a post-coital test. He explained that the "after-sex test" (post-coital sounds icky and weird) would be a simple swab of mucus from my cervical lining, no biggie, like Q-tipping a tiny gob of earwax. To me, though, this sounded scary and violating. I wanted to reach over and pull Josh close to my chair, but he already felt remote and distant, like I was slowly drifting off into outer space.

The doctor then told me about a dye test we should consider scheduling. I had heard of this test from a friend. She had firsthand knowledge. In her words, the dye going into me would feel like hydrogen peroxide on an open wound, except this wouldn't involve a quick stab of pain but a steady stream of burning agony passing through my Fallopian tubes. *No thanks*! I thought. *I'll pass on that test.*

The doctor then walked us through all the possible medications he might put me on, as well as the battery of tests and procedures he could perform on me to help us get pregnant. The key word in all this was *me*!

When the doctor finished what seemed to me like a too-lengthy harangue, Josh inquired about the expenses. The doctor asked us if we had infertility coverage on our healthcare plan. We nodded no. The doctor then shared with us how our total fertility costs would be largely contingent on two factors: how quickly my body responded to treatment, and how far we were willing to go to get pregnant. Best case scenario, we would pay seventy-five bucks for the first procedure, and afterward, we would get pregnant. Worst case scenario, we would pay twenty G's for an in vitro insemination (what the doctor called the "lobster," which sounded dreadfully painful to me because lobsters pinch. For Josh, "lobster" meant expensive, as lobsters are often the most pricy seafood item on the menu.) and still get zero return, as in nada, as in no baby, as in a goose egg (O) and not an embryo egg (XY).

I plodded out of the doctor's office in a daze. For the duration of the ride home, I said nothing to Josh. I was buried under an avalanche of doubt and fear.

The following month, I went in for the "Q-tip" test—the one the doctor said was "no biggie." He lied. The doctor's swab caused my pelvic region to tense and spasm. The nurse next to me tried to calm me down. "Just breathe through your vagina," she kept repeating, as though I had any idea what the H-E-Double Hockey Sticks she was talking about! The doctor finally snapped off his rubber gloves and gave up. He said we would try again next month.

Josh went back with me to the doctor's office. It didn't help. I failed the "Q-tip test" again. There was just something about the cold vinyl, my splayed legs strapped to bear-trap metal, and an object that looked like spaghetti tongs that made me freak out and resist like a pit bull. After the doctor left, I started weeping, while the nurse and Josh traded turns rubbing my back and letting me soak their shirts. Josh assured me that we would never return. I was done feeling like a mutant, being poked and prodded like a laboratory rat.

While Josh drove, staring out at the road with vacant eyes, I could feel the liquid anger turning into solid rage. *Why, God?* battered against my brain like golf-ball size hail. I couldn't dodge the pelting thoughts that because I had done everything by "The Book" (meaning the Bible), everything would naturally turn out for me like it did for Hannah with Samuel. Winding the tape reel all the way back to seventh grade, I remembered how I had read Elisabeth Elliot's book *Passion and Purity*—a book about pre-marital celibacy. As a result, I committed myself to abstinence until marriage and began wearing the cross-shaped purity ring, never once taking it off, even during the throbbing years of adolescence. And for what? Failure and frustration? Shame and humiliation? Outrageous medical costs and bleak fertility prospects?

On top of that, I thought of my job as a social worker, where I was assigned regularly to cases that involved dys-functional families, where one or both of the parents had bailed, or where the children had been removed from the home by the state because of neglect or abuse. And I thought, *How could God give children to people who would deprive them of love and comfort and safety, and then deprive people like me who would cherish and value and celebrate their children?* It just didn't make any sense. Nor did it seem just or fair.

At one point on our drive home, I turned to Josh and blurted out what I felt. It was like Mt. St. Helens erupting, spewing volcanic lava everywhere. "I just don't know if I can believe anymore in a God who would allow this to happen! It feels almost mean and cruel on his part. Don't you feel the same way?"

I didn't really want Josh to answer that question. He didn't. Instead he remained vice lipped and silent, allowing me to vent all the molten frustration inside. I felt relief for a moment, like the way one's stomach feels right after throwing up. But as the days passed and the salve wore off, I could feel the heartsickness creeping back into me like an advancing fog.

Disorientation

Josh

Amy and I had entered a season of disorientation.

We simply couldn't get our bearings. Our compass had failed us. We had lost our way. Like hikers who had confidently followed a trail cut with clearly marked signs, suddenly we had seen both the posts and the path disappear.

We now found ourselves crouched in the darkness, surrounded by menacing shadows, alone in the deep wood.

For me, disorientation meant not knowing what to do with my pain. Growing up, I had learned a lot of what it meant to "be a Bottomly man" from my grandfather, Colonel Heath Bottomly. Granddad grew up as a wild buck on the Montana plains. Granddad's stories of growing up on the Bighorn River meant more to me than my set of 1986 mint-condition Donruss baseball cards. My all-time favorite yarn involved Granddad's encounter with a grizzly bear.

When Granddad was ten years old, he had slept down by the river one night. In the morning, he awoke to the sound of a grizzly bear pawing at leftover strips of beef jerky. Waiting until the bear looked away, Granddad unzipped his tent and then made a mad dash for home. "Pa! Pa!" Granddad screamed as he came roaring through the front door. "There's a grizzly in my camp. Whatta I do?" His father didn't even look up from his morning paper. A long silence followed. Only Granddad's gasping breaths could be heard. Finally, his father crumpled the right edge of his newspaper, pulled his pipe out of his mouth, and, blowing a plume of smoke in the air, gruffly exclaimed, "Well, what are you doin' here? Go run that bear off! It's your campsite, isn't it?"

Returning to camp, Granddad led a flank attack, charging the bear from behind, throwing rocks, shouting like Davy Crockett, and sending the spooked animal gamboling off into the aspens. Granddad returned home as the valiant hero to claim his rite-of-passage badge from his father.

My story, however, went a tad bit differently. In my version, I failed the test, got mauled by the bear, and lost out on the badge.

Amy

For me, disorientation involved spooning down half gallons of Maggie Moo's cake batter ice cream, watching re-runs of *Gilmore Girls*, scouring eBay for designer jeans, or just letting the motion and sound of life's machinery droll on.

When Josh would come home from work, he would often find me curled up on the couch, wrapped like a mummy in my fleecy red blanket, hiding my puffy face and bloodshot eyes underneath my John Brown University sweatshirt.

Some days I would dream that I had simply disappeared.

During the acute times when I felt crummy, I'd call home or dial up a friend. "I know I sound like a broken record," I would apologize to them between heaves of tears, "but this is just the way I feel. I can't change that."

Specifically, I struggled to swallow the truth that I was now one of the 6.1 million women between ages fifteen and forty-four who were clinically infertile. Additionally, Josh and I were one of the 2.1 million couples who could not bear children. I had heard these disturbing statistics before on Oprah. I had watched Dr. Phil counsel infertile couples on their "alternative choices."[4]

Now I was one of Oprah's statistics.

Now Josh and I were that couple on Dr. Phil's couch.

At night, Josh and I would try to talk about our feelings. It was never easy. Sometimes we found it much easier to launch heat missiles at each other. The stupidest things would trigger a fight, like whether we should eat dinner out or in. What I failed to understand then was that while I couldn't see God in all my pain, I could see Josh, and that meant that I had an easy and open target. The times Josh tried to really listen and empathize with me, I could literally see his mind at work. He was like a screenwriter trying to cull through his thesaurus for just the right word. Often what came out of Josh's mouth fell fantastically short of Hollywood.

I knew that more than anything, Josh simply wanted to fix the problem. He couldn't. Later, I realized that what Josh struggled to understand was how he had somehow traded in one kind of impotency for another.

Most days, then, during our second year of barrenness, our marriage felt like a house that had lost its electricity during an ice storm. An ominous darkness silenced us. As the months drew out like a blustery Iowa winter, I became like an Eskimo, burrowed into my igloo of ice and cold and numbness. At night, though, during the dark and silent moments, I would find myself unable to block out one encroaching thought.

Everything felt like it had turned to ash.

Culp's Hill

Josh

The early months of 2006 equated to my "winter of discontent." My face had become, as Shakespeare aptly penned it, "full of frost, of storm and cloudiness."[5] I found myself living precariously in the space between *turning toward* God in radical trust and *turning away* from him in embittered unbelief.

I felt like I was on the verge of a spiritual breakdown.

I desperately needed a break through.

The next month God answered my plea.

While attending a leadership conference at Gettysburg, one night I was approached by Marty, a conference leader. He asked me if I wanted a personal tour of Culp's Hill, a famous battle during the Gettysburg campaign. I grabbed my Mountain Gear fleece; I was definitely up for it.

After snaking our way up through hills exploding with green April foliage, we stopped at a tiny knot of cedars surrounded by large boulders and scattered tree logs. "This was the Union army's extreme right position," Marty exclaimed as he pointed to a breastwork of cobbled stone covered in moss and dirt. "It was here that the fate of the Union army largely hung in the balance."

As Marty began to lead me around the markers that jutted up around the hill, the whole scene suddenly transformed before my eyes into a dramatic amphitheatre of war.

The main battle commenced at dusk on July 2, 1864.

As darkness moved in amongst the thick trees at Culp's Hill, the NY 137th disbanded in a thin line from the saddle down to the lower hill. Below the hill, gathering in a swale, and quickly filling up many trenches was a Confederate brigade led by General Steuart.

About that time, General Meade of the Union Army sent orders to Colonel David Ireland, the twenty-five-year-old commander of the NY 137th. General Meade's orders were short and exacting.

"Colonel Ireland, hold the line at all costs."

Soon Steuart's men moved into position behind the low stone wall in rear of the 137th.

They quickly unleashed a staccato of gunfire. Before they knew it, the 137th was taking heat from front, right flank, and rear. Their position, as Marty described it, was "like a finger, surrounded on three sides."

At about that time the 71st Pennsylvania regiment showed up. They were backups sent by General Hancock to assist the 137th. But seeing Ireland's men taking heavy musket fire from all directions, the 71st fired off a volley or two at Steuart's men and quickly withdrew from the line. Their position was untenable.

With half his infantry dead, resources depleted, and reinforcements in retreat, Ireland decided to order one final defensive tactic: commanding his regiment to stack up granite rocks to form a stone wall. There, entrenched on the saddle back between the hills, Ireland waited with his men.

As Marty showed me where Ireland had burrowed in with his men, I tried to put myself in the young colonel's shoes. I got down on my knees behind the stone wall and peered out into the thick darkness with only the silhouette of the overhanging limbs visible. I wondered how Ireland held his men together as trees splintered from canon fire, bullets pinged off granite rocks, and hot metal tore through sinewy flesh. I suddenly felt like I could hear the shrieks of young men as they breathed their last breath and their souls slid out of their bodies.

Somehow through the long and unrelenting night, Ireland and his men found the strength and fortitude to stymie every Confederate charge up the hill.

At around three AM, Steuart's men suspended their attack due to complete lack of visibility and thus an inability to determine who was who. They feared they were shooting and killing their own men. As their attack subsided, the 137th found renewed strength and hope as the 14th Brooklyn and the 6th Wisconsin showed up with reinforcements.

Had the Confederates known the 137th was the end of the line, they could have advanced toward the Baltimore Pike and overrun the Union army, changing the outcome of the battle at Gettysburg, probably turning the tide of the whole Civil War.

But the line never broke.

After Marty finished telling the story, I stood in complete silence, as I suddenly felt like Culp's Hill was becoming holy ground. I didn't see a burning bush or hear an audible voice. But as the wind rustled through the Pennsylvania birch trees and I stood against the cobbled traverse, I sensed somehow that God was near.

A scripture came to mind, one that I had memorized early in my life.

> Let him who walks in the dark,
> who has no light,
> trust in the name of the Lord
> and rely on his God.
>
> Isaiah 51:10a

For two years I had endured what St. John of the Cross called the *oscura noche*, the dark night of the soul. During that time, I felt like Job—confused, doubtful, and befuddled by God's seeming absence and deafening silence. My prayers were punctuated by sighs and groans. I came closest to God in my questions. I wondered not whether God existed but if God knew I existed. Did he know my pain? Did he see my suffering? Would he respond to my cry?

As I walked the hallowed grounds at Culp's Hill, I began to pray. Specifically, I echoed Peter's prayer: 'I do believe, Jesus, help me overcome my unbelief!' (Mark 9:24). I confessed to him that I felt like I was living within a precarious space between two parenthetical opposites: one being faith, the other being doubt. The bitterest pill I felt I had been forced to swallow involved watching Amy suffer and hurt and not knowing how to palliate her pain in any way.

In that moment, though, as the moon rose high into the starless sky and the leaves turned silver, I felt that God was near. For so long, God had seemed distant and remote, like a satellite. Sensing God's closeness now, I cupped my ear and leaned into the silence. What I heard filled me with a renewed trust that the night would give way to the day. And somehow, in some way, against all odds, pressed in on all sides, he would hold the line. Like Col. Ireland and the NY 137th, Amy and I would see the first gleam of dawn burst through the darkness. We would feel the sun on our faces again. We would hear a new word heralded through the clouds: a new day had arrived!

"You Too?"

Amy

When Josh returned from the Gettysburg conference, I could feel the lightness in him. Something had at least temporarily lifted. I still felt weighted down.

In late April, Josh and I received an invitation to Brandon's birthday party. Little did I know that Sherry, his wife, had schemed to bring me together with one of her friends, Melissa. Sherry thought we'd have a lot in common. When Melissa and I met, we quickly discovered that we did have something in common—our fertility problems.

C.S. Lewis once wrote that friendship often begins with "What? You too? I thought I was the only one."[6] For the next hour, Melissa and I had a number of "you too?" moments that immediately bonded us. Our conversations went something like this:

Amy: "I've struggled to be happy for girlfriends when they call with the 'good news' about their pregnancy.'"

Melissa: "You too?"

Melissa: "I've felt that because I haven't been able to get pregnant I'm behind in life, or missing out on that one thing that supposedly will make me feel 'fulfilled' and 'whole' as a woman."

Amy: "You too?"

Amy: "I've grappled to know where God is in all the frustration and failure and shame of my infertility."

Melissa: "You too?"

Melissa: "I even cried when I found out through *Us Weekly* that Katie Holmes was pregnant."

Amy: "You too?"

Before I left the party, Melissa asked me if Josh and I might want to join her and her husband, Chris, on Saturday for a Gladney adoption meeting. I had heard good things about Gladney from a friend who had put her baby up for adoption through Gladney years ago.

I said sure. I had not talked in depth with Josh about adoption. It had always been Plan B, or maybe C. Having biological children was always Plan A. However, with life's new extenuating circumstances, I went to the Gladney meeting with an open mind.

Sitting next to Melissa, I listened as our presenter, Lisa Elder, talked us through the different programs that Gladney offered. The last program Lisa presented was the Ethiopian track. It was brand new. In fact, as Lisa put it, it was still in its "pioneering stage." Immediately the program piqued my interest. I learned that the Ethiopia program was the fastest in the world and that one could adopt an infant under the age of one. The program required one short trip to Ethiopia, and very importantly, the Ethiopian program was the most affordable.

I walked away feeling like Ethiopia was our best option. Fast. Infants. Affordable. Those were three nice words that rang in my ears as the summer approached. More importantly, I felt like something was awakening, like a dormant seed suddenly exploding from its pod.

Jack Kerouac and Moonballs

Josh

As the end of the school year approached, I randomly tossed out an idea to Amy: what if we made all our married friends with babies jealous by packing a bag, pulling out the Atlas road map, hopping in our little Honda Civic, and just heading west? Freedom. Endless possibility. The open road. No boundaries of any kind.

I had just finished teaching Jack Kerouac's *The Open Road*, and obviously, I had been swept up in the electric, maddening hysteria that was the Beat Generation. The mere thought of driving across Route 66 through the night, feeling the arid desert air on my face, and pulling over just in time to watch the sunrise spill out into the cactus patches and outcropping of sandstone—it all left me quivering with excitement.

Amy was spontaneous enough to say yes!

Our first stop was in Colorado. I knew we could find free room and board with my parents. Our plan was to stay in Colorado Springs for a week (or two), then travel through Utah and down to Las Vegas. Although we originally planned to just go where the road took us, we ended up being more practical and mapped out where we would stop on what days. Amy was in charge of all hotel and camp reservations. Our plan was to work our way to the coast, hang out for a couple days in L.A., star watch in Hollywood, and shop around the Santa Monica pier. From there we'd work our way up Highway 1, where we would stop and camp in the Sequoyah trees at Big Sur. Then we'd bum around San Francisco, barking back at the sea lions off Fisherman's Wharf and smooching on top of Telegraph Hill, the spot overlooking the bay, where my mom and dad got engaged. Finally, we'd head back east on I-80, crossing through Nevada, stopping in Cheyenne, Wyoming, to see friends, and then ending our trip in Des Moines, Iowa—Amy's homestead.

One night at home in Colorado, I was poking around in my bedroom closet and dusted off an old shoebox full of childhood photos. Thumbing through the pictures, I came across one of me and my dad. It was a picture from my days playing basketball for the age ten-and-under Rockets. From the looks of things, I was going through a pre-pubescent phase, because I had missing teeth, beanpole legs, and short shorts so tight that my Superman underwear poked out underneath.

For a while, I just sat Indian style by the shoebox and relived old memories from that basketball season, remembering vivid moments in games where I'd heave the orange ball into the stratosphere of the Old Mustang gym, while Dad was yelling from the sidelines, "No moonballs, Josh! No moonballs!" (A moonball, by definition, was a shot taken from about twenty-five feet away from the basket.)

Suddenly, a distant and obscure memory from when I was ten bounced up and hit me in the head. It was a memory of a moment with my mom.

I must have been outside shooting hoops because I remember smelling of sweat and summer as I ran into the kitchen to get a drink of water. Before I went back outside, I went over and tugged on Mom's apron. She was cooking her famous beef stroganoff. She leaned over, and I whispered something into her ear that I didn't want my siblings to hear. "I've got a secret to tell you," I said, pausing for a moment to make sure Bow or Zak weren't trying to spy in on the conversation. "One day I'm going to adopt a little black boy."

Grabbing the shoebox and photo, I went out and asked my mom if she remembered me telling her about adopting a black boy. She tilted her head sideways and stared up at the popcorn ceiling, while her mind thumbed back through her sleeves of memories. Suddenly her pupils expanded. "Yes, yes," Mom exclaimed as she tapped the shoebox's lid I held in my arms. "As I recall, you told me about adopting a black boy, and I patted you on the shoulder and awkwardly said, 'Oh, that's really neat, Josh.' After you went back outside, I laughed to myself and thought, 'That was a little odd. Kids sure do say the darndest things.'"

During my stay in Colorado, I had told my parents about the Gladney meeting and our initial interest in Ethiopia. They listened respectfully, but I deduced from how quickly the topic changed at the dinner table that they didn't think I was that serious about it. Perhaps it was because I tended to talk a big game but never followed through with many things, like getting my Ph.D. Or maybe they didn't want me to get that serious about adoption. Secretly I wondered if what they wanted to tell Amy and me was, *Keep trying. We're praying for you. We just know you'll get pregnant soon.*

Later on I told Amy about the shoebox and photo, the memory with my mom, and my now twenty-year-old secret (adopting a black boy). I thought Amy would laugh at it all, but she didn't. In fact, she thought it might be a subtle sign.

That night, lying awake in bed, I was reminded of where Solomon wrote:

> God has made everything beautiful in its time.
> He has also set eternity in the hearts of men;
> yet they cannot fathom what God has done from beginning to end.
>
> Ecclesiastes 3:11

For all I know, I could have told my mom I wanted to adopt a black boy because at the time, I wanted to be black. I signed every spelling test in Miss Jackson's 4th grade class the same way—Kareem Abdul-Jabbar Bottomly. My bedroom was covered wall-to-wall with Michael Jordan posters. I regularly break danced in my silver glove to Michael Jackson's "Bad." If I could have brought two people to class for "Show and

Tell," I would have brought the two M.J.s. The reason was simple: I wanted to tongue-waggle and tomahawk dunk like one, and crotch grab and moonwalk dance like the other.

The other possibility for why I might have wanted to adopt a black child had to do with Solomon's insight. There are some desires inside all of us that we have no way of explaining because they border on the mysterious. To attempt with language to explain such a desire is like a parent trying to explain a solar eclipse to a child by comparing the phenomenon to a life saver.[7] Our language not only falls short, but it diffuses and strips that beautiful and mysterious event of its wonder and sublimity.

I tell my seniors on the first day of class that the books we read are not by accident. In other words, we don't choose the books we want to read, the books instead choose us. The question then becomes whether we will respect the book enough to listen to the secrets that it wants to whisper to us.

To this day, I believe that the faded photograph in the dusty shoebox at the back of the closet had chosen me. The photograph contained a memory that contained a secret. And though I had forgotten the secret about adopting a black boy, the secret had not forgotten about me. More importantly, the one who had whispered the secret had not forgotten about me. The question remaining was the same question I posed to my students: Was I listening?

Blog Days in Iowa

Amy

After we finished our romping adventures out west, Josh and I decided to spend the remainder of the summer in Iowa. It was an easy decision. We hated the sweltering humidity of August in Oklahoma, and on top of that, we knew my parents would spoil us rotten.

While Josh played golf with my dad and read books to prepare for school, I started spending long hours on the Internet, scrolling through pictures of Ethiopian orphans and reading blogs by adoptive parents. Every child's profile told a heart-wrenching story, often involving a parent dying of HIV or the strains of poverty causing desperate parents to abandon their babies on orphanage doorsteps. I probably looked at a thousand Ethiopian babies, and honestly, as I stared into their big, owl-like eyes and noted their exotic mix of Sub-Saharan and Middle Eastern features, especially their high cheek bones, light brown skin, and silky textured hair, I thought I could love, care for, and mother them all.

At the same time, I started battling anxiety about both Africa and adoption.

I had never visited Africa, and to be honest, the first thing that popped into my head when I thought of this continent was a song I sang in a musical with my church's youth choir. The song's chorus went:

> Please don't send me to Africa,
> I don't think I've got what it takes.
> I'm just a man, I'm not a Tarzan,
> don't like lions, gorillas, or snakes.
> I'll serve you here in suburbia
> in my comfortable middle class life.
> But please don't send me out into the bush.

The thought of the wild African plains, living out in a mud and straw hut, with flesh-sucking mosquitoes and meat-eating lions—yep! The song was right on: I didn't have what it took.

Along with my African fears, I felt stalked by adoption fears.

My years of social service work had provided a sobering portal into my possible future. For all I knew, my child could come with a sad history of physical trauma or emotional abuse. There could even be sexual abuse. I had been to enough training sessions to hear the disturbing statistics and learn about the newest psychiatric disorders amongst foster and adopted children.

I was in relationships with adoptive parents and knew from their stories what problems could be waiting for me around the next corner of life. In the blog world, I had read honest confessions of mothers suffering "post-adoption depression." I had learned that adoption was not an endless hot air balloon ride of euphoria. Many days, those moms wanted to scream, yell, kick, and even, if they could, go back and not go through with the adoption. Part of me found it hard not to be judgmental. How could parents feel that way about their adopted child? However, I knew what it felt like to censor words and emotions, fearful that if you were to be the R-rated version of yourself, your godly Christian friends would feel compelled to "share their concerns" with you. As I had learned through experience, most people preferred the G-rated version of me; it was safe, predictable, and convenient.

I had also read blogs of women who struggled with attachment issues. Months after adopting their child, there was still no bond. They had done everything the experts told them to do: held the child close to their chest, rarely let others hold the child, radiated sun-drenched love from their pupils, whispered soothing words, and rocked the child to sleep. And still, after all of that, there was zero connection with the child. This really scared me. The questions swirled around me like an Oklahoma twister: *What if I adopt and my child never connects to me? What if the child always treats me like an imposter mother? What will I do if the child constantly pulls away from me?*

In my most unguarded moments, I'd wonder if all my

questions and doubts were ominous signs of what was going to happen if we adopted.

Nothing dramatic happened to take away these fears. However, there were moments when I felt God's peace wash over me like an emerald wave. Those moments were not frequent, but they did happen.

I remember voicing some of my fears through Scott and Ann. They had adopted two children long ago, and they had lived through some turbulent passages across dark, uncharted waters. When I asked for their wisdom and experiential insights into adoption, they told me that all children involve risk, whether those children are biological or adopted. There were simply no guarantees. They knew Christian couples like we did who had raised their biological children to love God only to watch those children become prodigal sons and daughters, sowing their wild oats, making self-destructive choices.

Scott and Ann's insights helped me realize that all parenting was a precarious endeavor. Certainly adopting a child would involve a unique set of challenges, but all parents face their own versions of the gauntlet. What Scott and Ann shared with me was not necessarily something I didn't already know, but it was reassuring for me to hear them say it.

About that time, I started having a reoccurring dream of a little Ethiopian boy. Almost every night, a little black boy would just show up. When I would wake up in the morning and think about my dream, I would suddenly feel this strange goodness and sweetness on me, like morning dew. Although I had always wanted to adopt a little girl, I suddenly felt a seismic shift occurring at the tectonic plate level. Now, not only was I open to adopting a boy, but I was becoming oddly convinced that if it was true God sometimes speaks to people through their dreams, this was the closest thing I had ever experienced to hearing his voice.

At the end of August, Josh returned to Oklahoma City to begin the school year. I stayed behind in Iowa for a couple extra weeks. During that time, I felt the desire to adopt from Ethiopia grow firm, solid, and ripe, like Iowa corn in late summer. I remember calling Josh and telling him everything I felt inside, and little did I know, Josh had come to the same conclusions I had.

For the first time in our marriage, I began to pray with Josh. What was once an awkward activity was now seemingly effortless. Josh's prayers echoed mine. We both asked the Spirit to lead and provide for us. In addition, we asked for God to help us crush any lingering fears. Amazingly, I found my confidence growing not only in the Lord, but also growing in our marriage and in Josh. Perhaps for the first time I was beginning to discern why God had chosen me as Josh's Eve and Josh as my Adam.

Facing My Fears

Josh

Like Amy, I experienced a tumultuous stretch of days in August where I grappled with fear and doubt about Africa and adoption.

My most salient fears were fueled by thinking through the labyrinthine issues surrounding adopting a black child. I can vividly recall driving home from work and listening to an author on NPR argue that interracial adoption invited in too much confusion for all parties. Families like this would eventually erode underneath the "groundswell of cultural differences and ethnic barriers." As I listened, I began to feel uncomfortable. The author's words created a moment of fearful pause. I thought to myself, *maybe adopting a black child is taking on more than I can handle, especially in a part of the country where there are still large pockets of racism. Or perhaps the problems of prejudice are too big, the histories of injustice too long, and the feelings of bitterness too deep? How would I ever be able to explain to my son the slave trade and the eleven to thirteen million Africans who died at the hands of white people? What explanations would I conjure when my son came home from school with his American history textbook in hand and asked me to explain the images of burning crosses and children like Emit Till dangling from trees, burned to the bone and beaten to a bloody pulp? Or how would I assure my black son that the stares he felt in the mall or the racial slurs he might hear from the class bully at recess were not him, but them. In other words, how would I protect my son from America's most sordid and ugly sin—a sin that is tragically still very much alive in some enclaves of our nation?*

I remember Amy rehashing a story about one blog family who were adopting twins from Sierra Leone, and while out on a dinner date, a couple from their church approached them at the restaurant and publicly confronted them about the adoptions, forewarning them that "some things were never meant to mix."

Stories like that not only exacerbated my fears, but they also dredged up some belowground anger. I suspected that if some supposed "Christian" couple had reprimanded me like that, I would have introduced that couple to my altar ego, pulling out the baseball bat in the back of my car and going Joe-Pesci-in-*Goodfellas* on them.

However, during the two weeks when I was in Oklahoma and Amy was in Iowa, I experienced moments where God calmed my fears and spoke peace into my heart. One night I watched a short documentary film made by *Invisible Children* entitled "The Story of Emmy." The story is told by an American college student named Kenny, who travels over to war-tattered Darfur and meets Emmy, a ten-year-old boy. Over time, Kenny watches as Emmy's mother dies of AIDS, leaving Emmy an orphan. Fearful that Emmy has contacted HIV, Kenny agrees to take a blood test with Emmy at the local clinic. Hope springs up when both tests are negative. Pointing to their two vials of blood, Kenny tells Emmy, "You see, we're not so different, you and me. *We share the same color of blood.*"[8]

When the film ended, I found sudden and unexpected tears on my cheeks. One of the things I tell my students, which my mentor, Ken Gire, once told me, is that any time art touches your life with tears, whether through a story, song, film, or painting, it was wise to pay attention to those tears because your tears could help you find your heart. And if you found your heart, you found what was dear to God. If you found what was dear to God, you found the answer to how you should live your life.[9]

What I saw then, reflected in the distillation of my tears, was a dream that God had put down in the subterranean depths of me, so deep, in fact, that even a ten-year-old boy with beanpole legs could feel it. So deep, in fact, that nineteen years later, the same boy, now a man, could still feel it.

That night, I remember kneeling down next to my bed and lifting my palms toward God. I prayed two simple prayers. The first echoed Christ's prayer on Good Friday in the Garden of Gethsemane: "Not my will, but yours be done." The second prayer resounded with Easter morning's hope: "Lord, bring back to life what will please you and bring your name glory and advance your kingdom. Let it come in whatever form you desire. Thank you, Lord, for resurrection."[10]

The next morning, I took a stroll around my neighborhood lake to pray. While I sweated in the Oklahoma humidity, I began to ask for God's wisdom and guidance, and as I listened, what came to mind was the story of the covenant God made with Abraham and how in that covenant, God blessed Abraham so that all peoples on earth would be blessed through his seed. I confessed that like many American Christians I was good at Part A of the covenant (blessed by God) but lousy at Part B (to bless others).[11] To be in covenant with God then meant this: I had been chosen for the privileged responsibility of participating in one of God's many projects to bring order to the chaos on the earth, and more specifically, I was called to do this in the life of one Ethiopian child.

When Amy returned from Iowa, I told her I too was ready to move forward with adopting from Ethiopia. From the look of utter jubilation in her eyes, I could tell that an odd and strange marriage was taking place within our marriage.

Plan A

Amy

In September of 2006, Josh and I made the unanimous decision to adopt a baby boy from Ethiopia. I already had his name picked out. We'd call him Silas. I had always liked the name, largely because it wasn't in the Top 100 Most Popular Baby Names.

When we started telling our friends and family, I'll admit I was somewhat disappointed by the responses. The response I was hoping for was something like what Josh's brother, Zak, and his wife, Jessica, experienced when they had told Josh's family they were having a child. While on a mission trip in Rome, Zak and Jessica learned they were pregnant and decided to announce their pregnancy by taking a picture with tiny Jessica on Zak's tall shoulders, holding up signs that read: *We're Pregnant*! They gift wrapped this picture and waited until they returned to give it to Roc and Bev in front of the entire Bottomly gang. When Bev opened the gift and read the sign, she screamed and almost tackled Jessica with excitement. Roc, Josh's dad, squealed and bear hugged Zak. We all immediately jumped out of our chairs and mauled them like they were in the center of a mosh pit.

Our announcement moments, however, reminded me somewhat of the disappointment of our honeymoon. One couple I told could barely suppress their disbelief when they uttered, "Wow. We just never thought you guys would actually go through with it. I don't know what to say. Congratulations, I guess." It was responses such as this that made me feel like everyone secretly pitied us. Maybe I was a little oversensitive. Perhaps I was reading too much into their inflections. But what I felt was that our closest friends interpreted our plans to adopt as a consolation prize. I didn't win a first-place trophy but rather a commendable fifth-place ribbon.

Countless times after I told people about our plans to adopt, they would offer me their congratulations-slash-consolations by telling me stories of couples they knew who had infertility problems and decided to adopt, and then soon after adopting, surprise, surprise, they got pregnant. It wasn't hard for me to decode the hidden moral to their anecdote: God has a way of giving people back their dreams of biological children after they have taken a step of surrender to adopt.

What I wanted to tell these people was that adoption had become my dream.

Adoption was no longer Plan B.

It was Plan A.

After a while, it didn't matter to me how others might have felt. The more blogs I read, the more adoption pictures

I looked at, and the more articles I read about Africa, the more excited I became.

One blog I read was Abby Brown's. She and her husband, Ryan, had adopted a baby boy named Hennock. They now worked for Gladney in the Ethiopia adoption program. Abby and Ryan's adoption story not only inspired me, but it was one of the deciding factors in choosing Gladney for our adoption.

In February 2006, Scott Brown (Ryan Brown's father and Gladney's founder of the Ethiopian program) received news that Hennock was severely malnourished, weighing only five pounds. Ethiopian doctors quickly concluded that Hennock needed immediate medical treatment in the States. It was the child's only chance of survival. Scott and Monica heard about Hennock's condition and arranged everything with local doctors, telling Belay (Gladney's Ethiopian liaison) that they would take Hennock into their home, overseeing all medical procedures and costs. At the time, Ryan and Abby were living with Scott and Monica, and upon hearing about Hennock's situation, they instantly got swept up into the unfolding drama. When Hennock arrived in Fort Worth days later, Ryan and Abby helped transport the child to the hospital.

During the next two days, while Hennock received small dosages of nutrients like magnesium and potassium, Ryan and Abby both began to feel a strange shift occurring within them. Neither of them had talked about adopting or having children any time soon. All of Ryan and Abby's plans changed drastically within a span of only forty-eight hours. Before they knew it, their hearts had fallen in love with tiny Hennock, and days later, they agreed to adopt him. Neither Ryan nor Abby were remotely prepared for the deluge of paperwork, both from Gladney and the hospital, along with their new list of parental duties.

Through Abby and Ryan's story, I was able to get a glimpse into the hearts of the people working for Gladney's Ethiopian program. It helped me feel like I had already found a community of people who had a passion for orphan care. At that point, I was convinced we had found the right agency.

During the season of feverish anticipation, I went to blogspot.com and started my own blog. Before I knew it, I was playing and experimenting with my blog for hours, figuring out how to download pictures, create backdrops, and add posts. I loved the title of my blog: *Ethiopia or Bust*. It made me think of a balloon about to burst with too much helium. It was a fitting analogy for my internal state.

I wrote one of my first entries on Monday, September 11, 2006. The title of the entry was "We *are* adopting!" Here is a short excerpt:

> There is so much excitement in my soul right now! We have officially decided to adopt a baby from Ethiopia. The past year and a half has been very difficult slash disappointing, but I am feeling hope and peace right now. I am thankful … peace is good. Ahh … I just want to rest in this peace I feel.
>
> I am so eager to get the process started. I am so excited to see our future Ethiopian baby. I feel so excited that we get to adopt! I know not everyone

has this in their heart, but I am grateful that we have it in ours![12]

One thing I learned about having a blog was that a person can generate a faithful readership. It wasn't long before I made many new "blog friends." Most of my blog friends had either adopted from Ethiopia or, like me, were in the process. After many correspondences, I started making plans to set up "blog dates" with our husbands, taking our blog relationship to the next level.

Our first blog date took place in Dallas with Margo and Clayton Faulkner. Over Mexican food, we shared our story and let them tell their story. My favorite part of the Faulkners' account was how they had decided to adopt after hearing an inspirational message from a pastor at a conference in California.

Our second blog date was in Oklahoma City with a couple named Chris and Lisa Holliday. We instantly fell in awe with them. They were like a couple that could win the reality game show, *The Amazing Race*. Both were fit. Both were edgy. Both were avid outdoors people. During the dotcom boom, Chris made a killing, and to celebrate, he and Lisa took a year off and cycled down through Central and South America, covering almost six thousand miles. Although I loved the Hollidays' adventure stories, I equally loved their adoption story and their plans to adopt a sibling pair.

One highlight of our new friendship with the Hollidays' was discovering a local Ethiopian restaurant, the Queen of Sheba. Upon visiting the restaurant, we met Mimi and Begib, the Ethiopian owners, and immediately fell in love with them. It wasn't long before we were meeting the

Hollidays monthly at the Queen. We began to learn more about Ethiopia, as well as develop a palette and stomach for Ethiopian cuisine. I'll admit it took me some time to get over how much injera bread looked like human skin and tasted like a wheat pancake.

Over time, I began to realize that this adoption thing was about much more than just one child. It was about an emerging network of relationships, spanning all over the United States, connecting us to people who shared a similar passion along with similar pain. We were no longer alone. Instead we were becoming part of a growing, dynamic, and diverse adoption community.

At the same time but on a separate track, I was moving one hundred miles an hour as the self-appointed "adoption administrator" for all the Gladney stuff. Admittedly, Josh had zero organizational skills, so I put myself in charge of the dossier. This included tasks that ranged from gathering major documents like W-2s, birth certificates, and a marriage license to coordinating reference letters from pastors, friends, and employers, scheduling medical exams and fingerprints, and buying emergency tools like fire extinguishers.

Our Gladney worker, Andrea, had told me that the faster we got our paperwork in, the sooner we could have our Home Study, which meant the faster we would get our referral, which meant the sooner we'd travel to Ethiopia to get our baby boy.

In addition, I was able to participate in all the "first-time mom" stuff I had dreamed of doing. Friends like Sherry and

Erin came over and offered their decorating skills with our middle bedroom. Before I knew it, I was knee deep in color schemes and possible motifs. I wondered, *Should I go with a sports motif (Josh would like that), a cowboy-western motif, or an African motif?* It was so much fun to revel in the possibilities. In addition, when my girlfriends got together for lunch with their babies, I was no longer the lonely girl staring into my Caesar salad holding back the tears, but I was chiming in with my own anecdotes, feeling like one of the girls again.

A month later my parents visited, and I took them to my favorite baby store, Stork Land. When we arrived, my dad pulled out his money clip of cash and asked me what I wanted to buy. I was hoping he'd purchase me the crib I loved. He did more than that. Suddenly, our once barren and empty room had been transformed into a Pottery Barn-like baby's room, exploding with colors and a crib, a rocking chair, a dresser/changer, a closet full of clothes, and bins teeming with toys. Dad had bought all of it to bless me. When all was said and done, I felt like I had just been on an episode of *Extreme Makeover*, and Ty Pennington (my dad) had given me the baby room of my dreams. It was all too perfect. All the room needed now was a cute little baby boy named Silas.

A Kairos Moment

Josh

As we hurled excitedly along the adoption timeline, I found that there were moments of arresting beauty and hope, moments where everything stopped and stood still, moments where something divine slipped through the cracks of time and spilled out on me.

Down through the centuries, theologians and mystics have spoken of such experiences in time as *kairos* moments. By definition, a kairos moment is an event used by God to impact one's life. It involves an intersection of sorts between the horizontal and vertical, the humdrum and holy, where, for a fleeting moment, one experiences God's *nearness* in his life and God's *hereness* in his world.

Kairos moments have happened infrequently in my life. More importantly, kairos moments had never taken place for

Amy and me simultaneously. That was until a Sunday morning in early spring.

A friend of mine, John, asked if I would assist him at church and lead a corporate meditation on a psalm. About a month earlier, Amy and I had returned to church, but after eighteen months embroiled in a battle with infertility, I felt acutely disconnected from our local body. I didn't know how I'd reconnect with Bridgeway.

It's no coincidence that John assigned me Psalm 123, a psalm on the theme of suffering.

Here is what I shared with Bridgeway that Sunday morning.

The psalmist writes:

> I look to you, heaven-dwelling God,
> look up to you for help.
> Like servants alert to their master's commands,
> like a maid attending her lady,
> We're watching and waiting, holding our breath,
> awaiting your word of mercy.
> Mercy, God, mercy!
> We've been kicked around long enough,
> Kicked in the teeth by complacent rich men,
> kicked when we're down by arrogant brutes.
>
> Psalm 123

Ken Gire once told me that all good writers tell the truth—the whole truth. A writer does this by mustering the courage to open a vein.[13]

Psalm 123 is an example of a human being opening a vein. The psalmist writes in a language we all can translate and understand—the language of blood. Undoubtedly, blood speaks and connects to blood. When we tell the truth on this level, we not only connect to our own deepest humanity, but we also connect to one another's deepest humanity. At this level, we form a connective tissue of friendship not through our mutual sense of *wholeness* but through our mutual sense of *brokenness*.

While many of you knew of Amy's and my struggle with infertility, very few of you knew of the battles some of our friends had in our house church.

Our house church had gathered for almost three years. Our core was made up of five couples, all in their early thirties, all married, some with children, some without. When we gathered together, our conversations at the dinner table often bounced back and forth like a pinball between reality television, sports, and Hollywood gossip. It was easy for us to banter in one-liners from *The Office*; or debate who was better in football, University of Oklahoma or Oklahoma State University; or conjecture on who would break up first: Tom and Katie or Brad and Angelina. But when it came time to huddle up in the living room, read the Scriptures, and pray for each other, suddenly things would stiffen and go rigid. Often we could not get beyond the surface, both in God's word and in our own lives. By our own admission, we struggled to overcome our opaqueness.

By opaque, I mean to live unknown by others. It involves keeping one's life at such a frenetic pace that we become a blur of motion. Often we accomplish opacity in our lives by either A) staying perpetually busy, B) staying a safe distance from people, C) staying a safe distance from certain topics with people, or D) all of the above. While A involves our addiction to *speed*, B, C, and D involve our tendency to deal with suffering through *isolation tactics*. Whether it's with work or family, church or school, the Internet or television, we know how to move at a speed that keeps all of us detached and disconnected.

What contains the power to slow us down and move us toward each other again?

One word. One event, in fact.

Suffering.

In the past year, our house church had suffered intensely together. Our friends, the Sages, had endured an at-risk pregnancy with their twins. Doctors had told Brandon and Sherry they could lose one or both babies. One doctor, in fact, suggested terminating one of the twins. The chances of survival were small; the possibility of severe brain damage loomed large. For the last six months, the Sages had spent many days and nights vacillating like a pendulum between faith and doubt, hope and despair, the will of the doctor and the will of God. As a house church, when we prayed for them, we struggled to know how to pray, and in all honesty, we struggled to believe in the efficacy of prayer. Silence, on occasion, was our only form of intercession in the midst of their pain.

At the same time, another couple in our group, Abe and Gina, suffered a tragic death in their family. There were nights we held hands in prayer outside the ICU doors, petitioning God for Abe's father's healing, hopeful that he would bring about a full recovery. A few days later, though, our house church got a short e-mail from Abe. It simply read: "My father passed at one AM."

With one couple fighting for life, another couple grieving a death, and us reeling in our infertility, we suddenly became a community in travail. Literally, we were a "house of pain." Like never before, we found ourselves besieged by doubts and flanked by questions. Tacitly we all feared that the edifice of our faith would crumble.

What I came to realize was that our questions and doubts revealed that we were a community embarking upon a perilous journey. Like the Fellowship in *Lord of the Rings*, we had been led down into the mines of Moria, a place of eerie darkness and menacing enemies. We were undoubtedly traveling through a *terra incognita*, an unknown territory. To survive, we faced a crisis of choice: we could either turn inward and away from God and each other, or turn outward and open ourselves up to God and each other. There was no room for neutrality. It was an either/or dilemma.

Somehow, by God's sustaining grace, we found a way to move toward each other and let suffering transform us. Specifically, we discovered that we could crawl down into each other's hearts and just be there in the questions and doubts and fears.

It was possible to sit down with each other in the ashes.

Over time, something truly remarkable happened. We went from being people who simply believed in God to people who sacredly belonged to each other.

From *believing* to *belonging*.

There is a special fellowship in suffering. The apostle Paul knew this. That is why he exclaimed, "I want to know

Christ and the power of his resurrection and the fellowship of sharing in his suffering" (Philippians 3:10). We always prefer the resurrection part and not the suffering part. Most of our church services revel in the former and avoid much of the latter. But if we're honest, we know that community happens most profoundly during times of mutually shared pain. That's where we discover that community doesn't just happen; *it's earned.* Resurrection is the fruit that comes from sowing seeds of trust, patience, and perseverance with each other and God.

For Amy and me, the past two years has been our *via dolorosa*, our pathway of suffering, our cross. We have learned, though, that this path was a necessary prelude if the other word, the word of hope, which was the word that God had overcome the darkness, was to resonate more deeply in our hearts.

Today Amy and I are still without children, and without answers. We still find ourselves within the shadow of the cross. And yet we point to the cross in the midst of our infertility, and we exclaim with joy in our mouths.

This is the strange, odd, and beautiful place where we are called to gather. In our bodies. In our tears. In our questions. In our fears. And in our silences. We do this as a communal effort to proclaim: Through the cross and Christ's resurrection, God can transform our darkness into light, our brokenness into wholeness, and our ashes into new life!

A Note from a Stranger

Amy

I didn't know what Josh would share with Bridgeway on Sunday morning. After three years of marriage, I had only heard Josh speak once at the church, so this was still a side of him that I largely did not know. As Josh spoke, I felt a deeper sense of connection not just to his words but also to his heart. We had made our journey into the "unknown territory" of infertility together. In fact, we were still there. Many of our questions as to why we hadn't been able to conceive were still unanswered. However, our desire to know the answers had changed. I had wrestled with God like Jacob, and only after battling him through a long, Helm's Deep-like night had I made my peace. Perhaps peace wasn't the right word. Maybe it was more like surrender.

I was reminded of another conversation with Scott and Ann, in which I asked them if there had ever been a time when they felt "100% at peace with God" about not being able to have children. Ann replied, "You always wonder what it would have been like to have a child that looks like you and your husband. That curiosity never goes completely away. But you learn to trust God with the unanswered questions." At the time, Ann's honesty grated on me. I wanted the G-rated-Disney-movie answer, the one in which everything turns out okay in the end. Instead I got the R-rated truth. Now, though, I was beginning to realize the hard truth in Ann's words. Total peace, like all answers, may never come. They didn't for Jacob. Nor Job. Some questions remained unanswered even for Jesus, whether in the Garden of Gethsemane or on a Roman cross—"My God, my God, why have you forsaken me?" (Mark 15:34).

Ann's honesty then and Josh's meditation now helped me more fully to understand what Jesus meant when he said that I was called to "take up our cross and follow him" (Luke 9:23). Maybe just being human in all of my weaknesses and limitations was the cross itself. I don't know. What I do know, though, is that suffering works simultaneously as an *acid* that burns through our illusions of independence and also as an *adhesive* that binds us to each other in interdependence.

That morning, what Josh shared felt like a balm from the Lord. I believe it was also a healing ointment for others.

Afterward, Josh invited people to stand and receive prayer. Many did. As I watched as cells of people huddled up around those standing and listened to what sounded like a symphony of prayer, I thought to myself, *What a beautiful and compelling picture of God's people being God's hands, tears, and voice to those in pain.*

As I waited for Josh to finish praying with a few people, a woman slipped me a piece of paper with a note on it. I was surprised by this because I didn't know who the woman was, and I had never received an encouraging note from a stranger at church.

The note read:

> The one thing I know is that as long as you have that deep desire to have children, you will one day have them. One way or another, natural or adoption, he will fulfill that desire. And when he has given you the right number of kids, that deep desire will be replaced by a completeness never experienced before. So, hold onto that desire. Don't give up and know that his timing is always perfect.

Admittedly, I felt ambivalent about this note. In my experience, the theology of "personal desire and God's fulfillment" can be like spiritual dynamite, capable of blasting through ten-inch thick steel walls of despair but also capable of detonating prematurely and leaving only a bloody stump of faith. Take Abe's father, for instance. The desire of Abe's heart was for his father to fully recover from his heart attack, and yet, he died, leaving Abe feeling like a sinkhole had yawned open in his faith.

Placing the woman's note in my purse, I concluded that this note was tailored for my eyes. The woman's underlying intention was to encourage me with the truth that God not only knew every hair on my head, but he knew the trail of tears I had traipsed up the past two years. He knew the dreams inside my heart that throbbed and heaved in my rib cage.

Later, as Josh and I were leaving the church building, a man named Dave asked if he could pray for us. Dave's prayer was simple but sweet. He prayed that our child would be a leader and a prophet to his nation.

What was most interesting was that Josh did not share with the church that we were adopting, so neither the woman who gave me the note nor Dave knew we were in the adoption process. What was specifically amazing was that the note was not a letter attempting to discourage me from giving up on the dream of birthing children, but the note straight up mentioned adoption. Equally amazing was Dave's prayer that our child would be a leader and a prophet to *his nation*. Dave's prayer acknowledged both a boy and a different nation. Some may find this coincidental. Perhaps it was. But maybe God was letting me know that he was far more involved in all of this than I could possibly comprehend.

Later that night, as I reread the woman's note to Josh, he was reading through Frederick Buechner's book *Wishful Thinking*. Something in the woman's words prompted Josh to locate a passage in Buechner's book and read it to me:

"True vocation is where your deep gladness meets the world's deep need."[4]

Josh then read to me his notes scribbled in the margins next to the quote.

What Buechner was trying to communicate was

that I was never meant to confine vocation to my work, but that every facet of my life was meant to be fully integrated into my vocation. Vocation then is not necessarily what I do; it's who I am. Vocation, in other words, involved the deliberate act of living into one's fullest and deepest humanity.

For me, the combination of Josh's Sunday morning meditation, the woman's encouraging note, and Buechner's thoughtful quote was a single, integrated revelation that I was living at an intersecting point. My heart's deep-seated gladness was in the hope of becoming a mother, and the world's deepest need was the fact that there was a baby boy out there who needed a mother.

As I laid my head on the pillow, a smile crept across my face, and I thought to myself:

It's only fitting that an infertile *woman and an* invisible *child find each other.*

Perhaps, I concluded, *this is the most beautiful intersection.*

And it was coming very soon.

Waiting anxiously for Silas to be
brought to us for the first time.

Seeing Silas and finally getting to hold him.

Our "picture perfect" gotcha moment.

Family picture in Ethiopia.

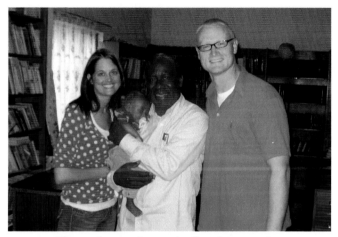

Pierre, the speaker at the Sunday morning
church service we attended.

Our amazing driver and friend, Tafesse.

Ryan, Abby, Enoch, and Marta Brown,
part of Gladney's in country team.

Belay, part of Gladney's in country team.

Africa

"As far as I am concerned, the greatest suffering is to feel alone, unwanted, unloved. The greatest suffering is also having no one, forgetting what an intimate, truly human relationship is, not knowing what it means to be loved, and not having a family or friends."

—Mother Teresa

"Pure and genuine religion in the sight of God the Father means caring for orphans and widows in their distress and refusing to let the world corrupt you" (James 1:27).

—blog entry by Jody Landers entitled "Why are We Doing This?" to explain why she and her husband, Andy, decided to adopt twins from Sierra Leone, Zeke and Kora.[15]

The Call

Amy

On Good Friday at 10:55 AM, my phone rang. It was an out-of-state area code. At that moment I didn't put one-and-one together.

The day before, Josh and I had made the trip to Iowa to celebrate Easter with my family. As we passed through Kansas City, I remember complaining to Josh that I thought the call from Gladney would never come. Josh reassured me that it would not be long. In fact, I remember Josh saying, "Wouldn't it be something if we got the call this weekend of all weekends, on Easter weekend?"

The next morning, my closest childhood friend, Gretchen, came over to see me. While we were catching up in the living room, my phone rang and I didn't answer it. The same number called again, and that time I interrupted Gretchen. I told her I just wanted to quickly check my messages. She knew that I was waiting for the call. My eyes dilated with excitement when I heard Mary's voice. It was our Gladney worker! I didn't even listen to half of Mary's message before I started nervously punching the numbers to return her call. As the phone began to dial, I started yelling at my parents downstairs and screaming for Josh, who was upstairs in our room. I could hear the thump and patter of their feet, one coming from above me, the other from below me. They converged with the same looks of anxiety mixed with nervous excitement.

I raced over with Josh to the laptop while my mom sprang for her camera. When Mary answered the phone, I instantly detected the giddiness in her voice. The first words out of her mouth were, "I have a very cute boy to show you." I screamed. Josh side-hugged me. This was it. Mary interrupted our enthusiasm to ask if both of us were sitting near a computer. I told her I had my laptop open and was ready for her e-mail. As Mary clicked the send button on her end, I stared unblinkingly at the screen on my end. I'll admit that I felt weird, like I was having an out-of-body experience. I tingled all over with I-have-no-idea-what-is-about-to-happen goose bumps. In a strange way, it felt like I was seeing my first sonogram, only in a much more Technicolor way.

"Oh, Amy, he's *so* adorable," Mary gushed. "His referral picture may be the cutest we've ever received." At that point I started to almost shake, as Josh started to do his nervous thing, biting his fingernails and spitting them out in between the couch pillows. At this same time, my mom started flashing off shot after shot like she was the paparazzi, trying to capture every moment in our state of suspended time.

Then a picture of a baby named Tesfamariam appeared

on the computer screen. My eyes blurred over immediately. I struggled to wipe away the tears fast enough to see his picture with clarity. Finally, everything came into focus. Tesfamariam was simply breathtaking. His big brown eyes, his tiny nose, his gummy smile, and his arms stretched out toward us like a teddy bear—it was all too surreal. Normally a mother's first image of her child looks something like a mix between a turnip and shar pei puppy, all wet and gauzy and purplish. Tesfamariam, on the other hand, was already a cute, cuddly doll.

Glancing over at Josh, I could tell he was beaming as a proud dad. He was all freckles and smiles. At about the same time, from just behind me, I heard a "Holy cow!" It was my dad. As he leaned forward over my shoulder, pushing his glasses up his nose, he suddenly belted out, "He's just so darn cute. I had no idea he'd be that cute." Nor did I. At times, during the months of waiting for our referral, I'd find myself, especially right before I would fall asleep, drifting off into that wistful place where I would take an imaginary brush, a palette of colors, and a blank canvas, and draw out a picture of what I had hoped my child would look like. Secretly, I had hoped for him to have big eyes, much like my own, and small, almost smurf-like features, so delicious that you just want to nibble on them. Tesfamariam was everything I had imagined and more!

After all of us had wiped away tears, blown our noses, and tossed one set of balled-up Kleenex only to grab another one, we sat quietly, so that I could listen with Josh to Mary as she walked us through all the e-mailed attachments. After she finished, Mary asked us to let her know in the next twenty-four hours whether we planned to accept the referral. I looked at Josh, already knowing his thoughts: *Can you imagine* not *accepting this child?* It was a no-brainer. Within twenty minutes, I called Mary back. "We'll take him!"

Afterward, Josh and I grabbed our cell phones and started calling family and friends. Josh was particularly frustrated because he couldn't get a hold of any of his family. I, on the other hand, was able to connect with my trio of best friends from college—Courtney, Cindy, and Sarah. "Girls, are you looking at your computers?" I asked, breathy with excitement. "I would like to introduce you to the cutest baby in the world: Silas Tesfamariam Bottomly. We plan to call him Silas." After their squeals and shrieks, they told me they wanted to know everything. I told them how Silas was born on December 29, 2006, and currently weighed nine pounds. At many points, the three girls couldn't restrain their joy, interrupting me and exclaiming things like, "He's such a long and lean boy!" and, "He's just so cute, Amy!" The rest of my conversation with my girlfriends involved lots of ooing and awing, especially over little things about Silas's picture, like the tiny freckle that dappled his nose or the little fist he made with his right hand. We laughed and cried, giggled and gushed, acting just like we did back in our college dorm room years ago.

Later that day, I told Josh how much I liked the name Tesfamariam. I had always hoped that I'd be able to pronounce his name in Amharic and that I would instantly love the sound of his name. Both my wishes came true.

I also learned in our information packet that Tesfamariam was a common Ethiopian name, one that his birth mother had obviously liked, and a name that reflected Ethiopia's Christian roots, particularly their Coptic orthodoxy. Interestingly, in Amharic, *Tesfa* meant "promise" or "hope of," and *mariam* translated meant Mary. Put together, Tesfamariam meant "hope of Mary."

That night, I nuzzled up close to Josh's pillow. I closed my eyes and saw Silas's smiling face, and as I did this, I could hear Josh quietly whispering to himself. He was quoting a psalm of David's that he had often shared with me during our most difficult days. David's words had brought me great comfort then. Now David's words brought me great joy.

I am still confident of this:

> I will see the goodness of the LORD in the land of
> the living.
> Wait for the LORD;
> be strong and take heart and wait for the LORD.
> Psalm 27:13

Little did I know the worth of our waiting. Although I had given lip service to David's belief in God's goodness, secretly I had struggled to really believe it. Now the Lord had answered the cry of my heart, even in my doubt and struggles with unbelief. He had caused a phoenix of new hope to rise up from the ashes. And he had allowed me to know his goodness in the face of a child named Tesfamariam.

Convergence

Josh

The months leading up to traveling to Ethiopia's capital city, Addis Ababa, involved a season of convergence.

It was like an invisible hand had taken the loose and disparate strands of our lives and braided them together into a single rope of unity.

As I shared at the book's beginning, our first year of marriage was extremely difficult. Our number-one "powder keg" topic was God. Often, our most explosive exchanges occurred after church or any time we tried to pray together. This, however, hadn't always been the case. Recalling our first breakfast date, I asked Amy to describe herself in five words. One of her adjectives was *missional*. When I asked her to explain what she meant by missional, it was like I had unscrewed the valve to a fire hydrant. I got blasted and sprayed with all her enthusiasm as she shared countless stories from her mission trips to Mexico and Ireland. It was obvious then that Amy's spiritual love language was missions.

When Amy asked me for my five words, I included the adjective *mystical*. Ever since I was thirteen years old, I have had this peculiar fascination with Christian mystics, like Brother Lawrence and Madam Guyon, and their spiritual quest for union with God. As a result, there was an "otherness" quality in me that Amy was drawn to like a magnet. And vice versa for me with Amy.

Amy and I had left our first date feeling an undeniable attraction to each other, and we had wholeheartedly sensed that if we married each other, we would make up two halves of the perfect spiritual atom.

A year later, however, Amy and I had found ourselves in the Manleys' living room, gnashing our teeth at each other. The mystical in me and the missional in her had brought the devil out in both of us.

The Manleys' advice: Put the "God stuff" aside for a while.

Amy and I had given each other furtive glances. That was borderline heretical advice. We had gone to Christian schools. We'd read all the marriage books. We'd seen the bumper sticker: "Couples that pray together, stay together." Not to pray together, not to read Scripture together, not to do church together—this was recipe for disaster!

Personally, I struggled with not feeling in sync with Amy spiritually. I fondly remember my family's summer vacations and traveling across I-40 west from Oklahoma City to Bakersfield, California, where my grandparents resided. What I recall most vividly were the mornings on the open road, where as the first yawn of sunlight reached up over the Sierra Mountains, I would wake up to hear my parents praying in the front seat, my mom praying in between gulps of steaming coffee, my father praying as he munched on a fistful of Mom's homemade granola. What always fascinated me was how smooth and effortless the act of praying was for my mom and dad. They were like two figure skaters gliding across the shimmering ice in perfect harmony. This was the kind of intimate relationship I ached for with Amy. Instead we spent our first years of marriage constantly slipping, falling, and crashing into each other on the ice. It felt hopeless.

Little did I know that God was answering the cry of my heart with Amy but in a creatively different way.

The first indication for me that we were beginning to find our groove spiritually was as we discovered books, blogs, and films on topics ranging from Africa and adoption to social justice and poverty.

I can still remember both of us watching the documentary *The Invisible Children* and being horrified by the Darfur genocides, and specifically, the cruel ways tribal gangs were using innocent children to conduct war and carry out mass murder. Amy and I immediately signed up to support Invisible Children's cause. We could give up one cup of Starbucks coffee to assist one Darfur child. It was the least we could do.

Soon after this, we read Tracy Kidder's Pulitzer Prize-winning biography, *Mountains Beyond Mountains*. Scott had given Amy a copy. Scott knew Amy would love it because he understood Amy's love language. The book told the story of Dr. Paul Farmer, a Harvard doctor, who had dedicated his life to curing diseases like TB and AIDS in third-world countries like Haiti and Peru. Dr. Farmer's life and message challenged us to move from an *emotional reaction* to the world's suffering to an *incarnational response* to the poor's plight. *Feeling* compassion for the poor was one thing. Frankly, it was easy. *Becoming* compassion in flesh-and-blood was quite another thing. It was much harder.

Soon the dynamics of our weekly B & N dates (Barnes and Noble) changed completely. Before, our dates had consisted of me reading books, Amy reading magazines, and both of us sipping on caramel macchiatos, barely speaking a word the whole time. Now, we showed up at the table with a stack of books on Africa, both eager to devour them like a stack of homemade pancakes. Interestingly, both Amy and I felt embarrassed by how little we knew about Africa. For example, of the fifty-three countries in Africa, Amy and I could only name eight—and that was counting Ethiopia!

Amy and I were amazed by Ethiopia's story of political autonomy. Specifically, we were surprised to learn how Ethiopia had staved off colonization by Western forces in the late nineteenth and early twentieth century. Briefly, in the 1940s, Mussolini and the Italians had invaded and occupied Addis, but a year later, they were ousted. In addition, we learned about the political upheaval in the 1970s, the Marxist revolution, and the cessation of the ancient monarchy. Notably, on September 12, 1974, three soldiers came to Emperor Haile Selassie's palace, put him in the backseat of a Volkswagen Bug, and took him to prison. Following Selassie's usurpation, Colonel Mengistu, a commander of the Derg army, assumed power and ordered his men to execute the emperor's imperial guard, along with a large group of parliamentary leaders. Emperor Selassie died a year later, either due to cardiac arrest or suffocation with a pillow. For almost twenty years afterward, the Derg ruled, shutting down Christian schools, removing Christian symbols, and forcing all Christian churches to operate underground.[16]

One of my colleagues had actually lived in Addis during the height of the Marxist revolution, a period later called "The Red Terror." He and his wife had taught at an international school in Addis. He told me stories about how they lived for a year under military-mandated curfews and that they were only allotted enough gasoline to drive to work and the grocery store once a week. We later learned from them that the military executions of Selassie's royal guard took place only a mile from their house, and in fact, they saw the furrowed-out ditches where the bodies were later piled up and buried.

Amy and I became zealous students of all things Ethiopian, assiduously soaking up all knowledge like a couple of dry sponges. There were nights I'd come home from work and find Amy's nose wedged between pages 250 and 251. She'd be sitting on the couch—the same couch she had once spent months curled upon in agonizing sadness—swallowing whole books in days like a female python. One book Amy read was *There is No Me Without You*, by Melissa Fay Greene, which tells the story of Mrs. Haregewoin Teferra, a middle-class Ethiopian widow whose home became a refuge for hundreds of AIDS orphans. Frequently, Amy would look up from her book and interrupt me in mine, only to rattle off a staccato of statistics phrased in the form of rhetorical questions:

Amy: "Did you know that 81% of Ethiopians live on less than $2 a day?"

Josh: "No, I didn't."

Amy: "Did you know that by 2010 experts anticipate that there will be between 25 and 50 million orphans?"

Josh: "Wow! That's, like, over ten times the population of Oklahoma City!"

Amy: "And, Josh, get this, did you know that if we snap our fingers every three seconds, another child has died of a preventable disease?"

One … two … three … snap! One … two … three … snap! One … two … three … snap![17]

There were many nights thereafter when I felt overwhelmed by such harrowing statistics. Instead of feeling the horror in my guts, I'd feel nothing. The more I learned, the number I became. To stave off the hidden anesthetic within these statistics, I would sometimes stop and pray simple prayers of intercession. I knew God grieved over this, and he wanted me to feel something of his heart for the suffering peoples of Africa. More importantly, God wanted me to become his heart for the abandoned and neglected orphans in Ethiopia.

One salient memory I have with Amy involved watching *Hotel Rwanda*. The movie tells the story of one man's courage in the face of the Rwandan genocides, where members of the Hutu tribe killed over 800,000 from their rival tribe, the Tutsi tribe. After the movie ended, I felt disemboweled and sat in stunned silence with Amy for a long time. The Rwandan genocides had occurred when we were seniors in high school, and yet no one had ever brought it up. Neither Amy nor I could recall one prayer request for the Rwandan peoples, let alone a prayer vigil at our churches or schools. Instead, we attended Bible class each day, and after the daily devotion, we prayed for Aunt Maud's sore toe, along with the smattering of "unspoken" prayer requests. All the while, nearly a million innocent men, women, and children were being butchered to death by Hutu machetes.

Just how ignorant I was began to hit me, and specifically, how insular my life had been up to this point. I also began to realize that for Amy and me, God was not only moving us *toward* each other and *into* each other's hearts, but he was also moving us *outward* into a bigger world, a world ravished by stupid poverty.

And what was stupid poverty? Four months earlier I couldn't have told anyone the answer. But thanks to books like Kidder's *Mountains*, along with others like Ron Sider's *Rich Christians in an Age of Hunger* and Tom Davis's *Red Letters*, I now could. And if I had uncovered a common thematic thread woven through all of these books, it was that s*tupid poverty existed in many parts of the world because of sinful human choice.*

I also learned that stupid poverty had very concrete manifestations. They were easy to spot and detect, but most people were choosing not to look close enough to truly see them.

Stupid poverty was *hunger*.

Stupid poverty was *illiteracy*.

Stupid poverty was *disease*.

Stupid poverty was *brain damage*.

Stupid poverty was *mortality*.[18]

And stupid poverty was where God was, and sadly, most of the evangelical American church wasn't.

I'll never forget reading an interview with Rick Warren, author of *A Purpose Driven Life*. In the *New York Times* article entitled "Evangelicals a Liberal Can Love,"[19] Warren acknowledged that for most of his life he wasn't much concerned with issues of poverty or disease. But on a visit to South Africa in 2003, he came across a tiny church operating from a dilapidated tent yet sheltering twenty-five children orphaned by AIDS. "I realized they were doing more for the poor than my entire mega church," Mr. Warren said, with cheerful exaggeration. "It was like a knife in the heart." As a result, Warren mobilized his vast Saddleback Church to fight AIDS, malaria, and poverty in sixty-eight countries. Since then, more than 7,500 members of his church had paid their own way to volunteer in poor countries, and once they saw the poverty, they immediately wanted to do more.

I thought, *Now here is an evangelical leader I can follow. But at the same time, I wonder how many other evangelical Christians would follow Warren and his message versus how many American evangelicals would abandon ship, choosing to hop on board with pastors who offered them a more popular brand of the Gospel—one that was much more privatized, feel-good, hyper-individualistic, and consumer-driven.*

I'll also never forget watching Bono's NAACP acceptance speech. Amy found it through a friend's blog. Bono's speech was primarily on Africa, the AIDS crisis, and the call to Christians to embrace a theology of social justice. Earlier, Amy had shown the video to her mom. Joyce had always had her suspicions about U2's lead singer. "Do you think Bono really is a Christian?" Joyce had asked me once. I could sympathize with the source of her question. Bono drank, smoked, and used the F-bomb. He even dressed up occasionally as the devil and pranced around stage with horns and a pitchfork. How then could a cigar-toting, cussing rock star be a prophet and preacher?

Bono's speech answered Joyce's questions. In fact, when we all walked away, we weren't questioning whether Bono was a Christian, but if we were. At least, I know I was.

For me, the last part of Bono's speech was the most challenging and moving.

> God has a special place for the poor. The poor are where God lives. God is in the slums, in the cardboard boxes where the poor play house. God is where the opportunity is lost and lives are shattered. God is with the mother who has infected her child with a virus that will take both lives. God is under the rubble in the cries we hear during wartime. *God is with the poor and God is with us if we are with them.*[20]

One of the things I had wrestled with prior to Bono's speech was the financial aspect of our adoption. I had learned by experience that Christians in my generation believed that topics like sex or politics were okay, but when it came to the topic of money, there was an unspoken rule about it. Some things were private matters, and money fell squarely into that category. As a result, I didn't broach our adoption expenses with many people, even within my closest circle of friends and family (although I discovered that strangers would ask me: So how much will adopting a child cost you? $10,000? $20 grand? $30 Gs even? One could easily have overhead our conversation and thought we were talking about cars, not children).

When it came time to figure out how I was going to finance the adoption, I looked over our assets and bank statements, and I knew we were going to be shortchanged in a major way. Most unsettling was the prospect of new debt. After years of languishing in the red financially, we had finally scraped and saved our way back into the black. Amy and I had learned how to budget our monthly expenditures, live responsibly within our means, and even save money for emergency contingencies. We were living debt free except for our house. Within a few months, though, we found ourselves staring back down the barrel of loan debt for a very long time, where just paying the interest alone would be a challenge.

We had known other couples who had written support letters and raised money to cover the expenses. For whatever reason, though, Amy and I felt reluctant to do this. Moreover, I personally felt like adoption fell into a real "gray area" for many Christians. The reason was because adoption doesn't really fit the "missions" category as most churches define it. Amy and I weren't going "over" to a country, sacrificing our comfort and safety in order to meet the needs of an indigenous community, whether by building a church, providing medical assistance, or proselytizing to the lost. Instead we were bringing a child back from a country into our home. Moreover, while children in America cost money, in third-world countries, children make money for their family's survival.

So who then really benefits from an African adoption?

Sometimes I could sense what some people tacitly thought: *Well, yes, you guys are reaching out to a needy child in Africa, but you are also getting something in return for that child—specifically, the satisfaction of being parents. So it's a win-win deal. The child gets a home, and you get a child. So can you in good conscience seek to solicit charitable monies from anyone?*

Hidden questions like these shadowed me. I feared that I would cut myself on the dangerous edge of compassion because I wanted to adopt for the warm buzz it would give me, either palliating my personal pain or filling a personal hole. In all truthfulness, I don't know where the line between my selfish needs end and my sacrificial love begins. I may never get clarification. What I tried to keep front-and-center throughout the financial process was scriptures like James 1:27, along with the forty other scriptures on God's heart for orphans[21], and reminded myself almost daily that if there was a kind of consumer debt that God would endorse, it would be compassion-centered debt.

Through Bono's speech, though, I sensed that the Lord's word to us was Jubilee. Leviticus 25 came to mind, and I was reminded that every fiftieth year in the Jewish calendar, all Israelites were to dismiss any outstanding debt. All loans were to be cancelled, all land restored to the original owner, and all slaves freed to return home. Interestingly, I had never heard of the Jubilee year growing up. Bono, in fact, was the first to introduce me to Jubilee through his song "Beautiful Day," which was a song written to celebrate the 430 million dollars of debt that the U.S. canceled in loans to Africa, a cause Bono had been championing for years.[22]

Much later, Amy and I heard a radio talk by Dr. Dobson on adoption. He told his own story of how he and his wife, Shirley, had adopted their son, Ryan. After sharing this, Dr. Dobson told Christians it was not okay just to give money to their church. They also needed to help financially with those who had a heart for adoption. Dr. Dobson didn't stop there. He also implored Christians to consider adopting a child into their family. His message was simple: *Adoption is one way we can more effectively evangelize our world.*

Both Amy and I were encouraged by Dr. Dobson's compelling message to evangelicals. Personally, I sensed that God would provide for us, maybe not in a hailstorm of manna from the sky, but he would take care of us, and as Bono put it, "have our backs."

One of the things Amy came to immediately love about Ethiopian culture was their practice of compassion. She had learned in her research that it was Ethiopian decorum at public restaurants to leave a small portion of the meal on the plate. That uneaten portion was then given to the poor. Moreover, Amy learned that many Ethiopian Christians fast regularly, sometimes as many as 210 days of the year. Later, I read a disturbing statistic that one American eats what 520 Ethiopians eat in their lifetime.[23] The tragic reality was that while America has reality shows like *The Biggest Loser* and a national obesity crisis, Ethiopians had famines and suffered from a starvation crisis. More disheartening, Amy and I discovered that American Christians spend four times as much each year on dietary programs as they do on humanitarian aid.[24] This miscellany of statistics jettisoned Amy and I toward incorporating fasting more intentionally into our lifestyle. We began to use our breakfast or lunch on Tuesdays for intentional prayer for the orphans in Ethiopia. Specifically, we shaped our mouths around the words of the prophet Isaiah:

Is not this the kind of fasting I have chosen:
to loose the chains of injustice and untie the cords
of the yoke,
to set the oppressed free and break every yoke?

Isaiah 58:6

Notably, I had always thought fasting had to do with developing a more ravenous appetite for God. But now I was beginning to learn that the prophetic purpose behind fasting was full immersion into the human condition. In other words, *fasting was about total involvement in the suffering of the world.*

Passages like Isaiah 58 only piqued my curiosity to reread the Bible in effort to rediscover God's heart for the poor. It wasn't long before I began to take a highlighter and mark passages that had to do with the poor. Starting in the Old Testament, I learned about God's provisions for the poor, ranging from the practice of gleaning (Lev. 23) to the year of Jubilee (Lev. 25), from interest-free loans (Lev. 25) to the year of the tithe (Deut. 26). I also worked my way back through the Gospels, specifically highlighting all the passages on the poor, ranging from Jesus' Nazareth manifesto (Lk. 4:18–19) to the Beatitudes (Matt. 5:3–12), from his parables on the Good Samaritan (Lk. 10:25–37) to his eschatological story of judgment (Matt. 25: 31–40).

Undoubtedly, the Bible was becoming like a book I had never read before.

There were many times then when I found myself scratching my head in utter befuddlement at how I could have missed over 2,000 passages of Scripture that had to do with a stark cornucopia of themes in the Bible related to poverty, compassion, and social justice.[25]

There is a truism in education: "All true learning is caught, not taught." From age thirteen on, I was infected by my Bible teachers with an ardent zeal for the word of God. By the time I graduated from high school, I had memorized the Sermon on the Mount with Mr. Sciacca, performed inductive studies on books like I Peter, Romans, and Revelation with Kay Arthur (at Precept Headquarters), and imbibed on the best expository teaching in the world with my father. And yet, in all honesty, I recognized that although these spiritual mentors passed onto me significant pieces of a biblical worldview, there was one vital piece that they failed to give me—the piece in the Scriptures that draws attention to God's stance toward the poor. I wonder now how my worldview might have changed if growing up, I would have learned about the God who "upholds the cause of the oppressed" and "watches over the alien, and sustains the fatherless" (Ps. 146:7, 9), the God that requires us to "take justice to the public streets"[26] (Am. 5:15) and a God that came to earth on a mission to "preach the good news to the poor" (Lk. 4:18), a God who explicitly tells us that those who neglect the poor and oppressed are not God's people at all (Isa. 1:10–15, Matt. 25:31–46).

As May rolled around and Amy and I boarded the plane for Addis Ababa, I had this deep down intuitional feeling that our time in Africa would equate to crossing the Rubicon and passing beyond a point of return. Both Amy and I were excited and terrified about this. But what we jointly celebrate to this day is how the combination of reading books, watching films, and rereading Scripture in lieu of themes related to the poor helped both Amy and me *reorient our lives around a personal relationship with Jesus and a public mission into the world.*

Ethiopia or Bust

Amy

I'll admit that among the host of things that frightened me—including basements, gynecologists, breast cancer, tornados, and the dark—flying ranks right up there with Pike, the basement serial killer from my childhood.

Months before I even received our referral, I actually called Mary, our worker, and asked her if Gladney had some kind of escort service. I thought maybe there was a way we could cut travel costs, along with avoiding a terrorist attack or plane crash in the Atlantic or Sahara. I believed my arguments seemed compelling and airtight. Mary, however, wasn't sure if I was being serious. She'd never had this request before, and from what she understood, escorting was only for emergency cases. I obviously didn't qualify. Darnit!

The good news was that the more I learned about

Ethiopia and the more excitement grew, the less afraid I became of flying. More importantly, it had been many years since I'd traveled to a third-world country, and as the days approached our trip, I felt something percolate in my blood that I hadn't felt for a long time. What it was I couldn't put my finger on, but it definitely put its finger on me. It had something to do with my longing for missions and my love for the poor. Both missions and the poor were like double helix strands that made up my basic spiritual DNA.

In Washington, D.C., Josh and I met up with Clayton and Margo Faulkner, our Dallas blog friends. They were going over to Ethiopia to pick up their adopted boy, Deacon. Upon boarding an Ethiopian Airline plane, I was excited to discover Ethiopians on all sides, many dressed in colorful shawls, all exotic looking, and eager to return to their home-land. We stood out like sore thumbs.

I had specifically prayed for God encounters throughout our entire trip. I hoped that our time in Addis would link us up with a broader network of people who had a heart for orphans. Not long into our flight, a little Ethiopian boy zoomed by our row like a Tasmanian devil. He was the cut-est thing, and I immediately became curious as to who his parents were. A white woman snatched the boy up from the aisle, wrestled him into his seat belt, and offered him an ani-mal cracker as a peace offering.

Curiously, I poked my head around my seat to see who was sitting next to the woman. Instantly I was excited to discover her husband, also white, using his arm as a pillow for one of his three boys, all sprawled out in the other seats, conked out. The couple had four boys, two white and two black. The parents looked young and hip, perhaps in their late twenties or early thirties like us.

Eventually I introduced myself to the couple. Their names were Tara and Ralph Leo. They were traveling to Zimbabwe for six weeks. Ralph was planning to teach a theology course at the local seminary. When I asked them about their adoption story, Ralph prefaced his part by telling us how excited he was that we were going to get our "faith violated" in the coolest way. "Faith, as we have learned," Ralph exclaimed, "is spelled R-I-S-K." I'll admit: Ralph's little disclaimer stirred up ambivalent feelings within me. Words like *faith, risk,* and *trust* sounded great when they were spoken from the church pulpit and received from a comfortable pew, but when you're 25,000 feet above a great big body of water and on your way to doing something a little bit crazy, those same words become a little less inspiring and little more frightening.

To hear their story was spine tingling.

In the fall of 2006, Ralph and Tara had completed all the adoption paperwork for a three-and-half-year-old boy named Kirubel. Two weeks before traveling to Addis, Ralph and Tara went to dinner with a family, the Knudsens, who had four children of their own (two biological, two adopted from Ethiopia). During the meal, the Knudsens asked Ralph and Tara to pray for a three-year-old who was living in the same orphanage as Kirubel, who suffered from a retinal blastoma in his left eye. Earlier the boy had been matched with an American family, but when the family learned that the boy had a tumor in his eye, they denied the referral. The

Knudsens did not know anyone who could intervene and help, but they knew that Ralph and Tara were Christians. So they asked them to at least consider meeting the boy at the orphanage. Later Ralph and Tara learned that Wide Horizons, their adoption agency, was trying to get the boy a medical visa so he could be treated in the United States. However, the U.S. did not allow medical visas for orphans.

On the flight over to Addis, Ralph felt God speak to his heart and say, "You are going to bring this little boy home. He will be your son." After arriving and meeting their adopted son, Kirubel, they immediately asked the staff where the boy with the tumor was. The man in charge, Dr. Tsegaye, led them over to a crib where a boy was sleeping. His name was Getu. Tara and Ralph asked Dr. Tsegaye what they planned to do for Getu. The doctor grimaced with a forlorn expression. Suddenly, without thinking or asking Ralph, Tara just blurted out, "Well, could we adopt him?" Somewhat shocked, Dr. Tsegaye looked at both of them and replied, "Well, technically it would be best if it was a family like you because all of your information is updated, but you will have to come back in a couple months. It will take that much time for all the paperwork, specifically the visa and passport, to be processed." That night Tara and Ralph felt a strong sense from the Lord that Getu's paperwork would be processed expeditiously by the time they left the following Friday. They prayed together for a miracle. A week later, Getu was on the plane back to the United States, all his paperwork completed, legally the adopted son of Tara and Ralph Leo.

Three days later, doctors at Boston Children's Hospital removed Getu's left eye. The tests revealed that they got the cancer just before it entered Getu's brain. For six months after, Getu returned for weekly check-ups, and doctors continued to find no evidence of any cancer. No chemo or radiation was ever needed.

A funny side story Tara told me about Getu was that his picture appeared in *Star* magazine two weeks later. Supposedly, Getu is related to Zahara, Angelina Jolie and Brad Pitt's adopted daughter. Because the media couldn't get a picture of Zahara, they decided to print the next best thing, a picture of Getu.

Before I departed the plane, I exchanged e-mails with Tara, and still today, we stay in touch. What I took from meeting Tara and hearing the story of Getu was that there were others out there who shared a similar passion for Africa and orphans.

After we arrived in Addis and went through customs, we met Belay, Gladney's in-country administrator. He was bigger than his profile picture. My first impression of Belay was that he looked like a big brown teddy bear.

As we waited for our luggage at the baggage claim, we quickly learned that Belay loved to tell anecdotes and crack jokes. "Once, a little American girl saw me, pointed me out to her mother, and exclaimed, 'Look, Mommy, there is an Ethiopian that isn't malnourished like you told me. He *obviously* hasn't skipped a meal in a very long time.' "Belay's laughter at his own story caused his plump belly to roll like waves at high tide. I giggled and knew I would love Belay's company.

Later, I learned that Belay's story was earmarked by tragedy early on; his father was executed by the Derg during the Marxist revolt in the 70s. His father was the chief officer of Emperor Selassie's royal guard. The day after Selassie was removed from his throne, Belay's father, along with sixty top officials of Selassie's government, were taken to an empty area just outside the prison and mass executed. Belay's mother was also imprisoned for eight months. Belay came to the United States in 1981 and found amnesty. Belay and his family lived in Texas, where Belay matriculated to college, and after many successful years in business in California, he decided to return with his family to Ethiopia. Both he and his wife wanted to raise their children in their homeland, and Belay in particular desired to use his education and professional skills to assist his fellow Ethiopians.

Soon after returning to Addis, Belay connected with Scott Brown, Gladney's chief financial officer, who had ambitions to start an Ethiopian program with Gladney. Belay was Scott's first hire in country.

I contribute much of our friction-free adoption experience in Addis to Belay. He was like a benevolent version of Tony Soprano, a man with government connections, capable of running interference and cutting through red tape.

One of my chief concerns was the amount of corruption involved with international adoption. I had heard horror stories of people who had been ripped off and extorted by the greedy machinery behind most African governments. Meeting Belay quelled all my fears. If ever there was a Moses figure leading us through the Red Sea of government procedure, it was he.

After getting our luggage, Belay introduced us to our driver, Tafesse. My Washington, D.C., blog friend, Anne, had recommended Tafesse. She and her husband, Mike, had traveled to Addis a few months prior to us to pick up their adopted girl, Lilly. Part of what made Anne and Mike's trip so amazing was having Tafesse as their driver. He was not only a safe driver, but he was intelligent, spoke perfect English, and even got American jokes. By the time Anne and Mike left Addis, Tafesse was like family.

As Tafesse drove us to our hotel, we introduced ourselves to him and passed along Anne and Mike's hello, which gave us instant credibility with him. It wasn't long after this that Tafesse began to educate Josh and me on Ethiopian culture. He explained to us that Ethiopians were very proud people, and that like Texans, they identified themselves separately from other Africans. We had heard that Ethiopia had never been colonized, but Tafesse reinforced how proud Ethiopians were of this fact and that the country's political autonomy was reflected in everything from their language (Amharic) to their calendar (Ge'ez). As we passed by our hotel, Tafesse pointed to a billboard that read: The Countdown to the New Millennium. Seeing our puzzled faces, Tafesse laughed and then explained that in Ethiopia it was 1999, and that in a little less than six months, Ethiopia would have a huge celebration with festivals and parties to usher in the next century. I asked him jokingly if he feared the Y2K bug. I didn't think he would get my humor. Tafesse wagged his finger and laughed.

Stepping out of the car, I immediately scanned my eyes around the collar of mountains that surrounded me. The air felt crisp and smelled of ripe bananas mixed with carbon plumes. Tafesse pointed out the highest point in Addis, the summit of Mount Entoto, which was 3,200 meters above sea level. We could barely make out the mountain's frame, catching only a glimpse of the summit's jagged silhouette flickering through the phosphorescent streetlights.

Our hotel in Addis was absolutely gorgeous. It was surrounded by aquatic fountains, botanic gardens, and marble pillars. I looked over at Josh and gave him a look like, *Are we on our honeymoon or what?* (The one I had always imagined.) Earlier, I had argued with Josh over where we would stay in Addis. We had three options. We could either stay at the Sheraton, the most expensive hotel in Addis, stay at the Hilton right across the street, still expensive but not as extravagant, or stay in the Gladney guest house, the cheapest and most affordable option. Thinking back to our honeymoon and Josh's choice of the lizard-infested pink shanty, I took charge of our travel arrangements. Although I knew we could cut costs by staying in the guest house, I felt that because Josh and I were going to be first-time parents and were in a foreign country, it would help if we had a little oasis to return to each day. We knew the Sheraton would provide us this. So we ruled out the guesthouse, looked into the Hilton, and agreed on the Sheraton. Rough, huh?

After we settled into our amazing room, Josh ordered room service, and we celebrated our last night as a childless couple. Admittedly, it all felt a bit surreal for me. I couldn't believe that in less than twelve hours I would be a full-time mom, solely responsible for a little human life. Gulp!

That night I tossed and turned with excitement and anxiety.

Silas Day!

Josh

The next morning, Tafesse picked us up at nine AM sharp. Coming out the hotel door, I frantically checked off the bazillion baby items.

Bottles, nipples, and formula: Check.

Diapers and wipes: Check.

Six onesies (for six spit-ups): Check.

Socks, shoes, and sweat shirts: Check.

Rattles, toys, and pacifiers: Check.

Camera, video recorder, and batteries: Check.

Snacks and water bottles: Check.

Baby Tylenol, Band-Aids, and gauze pads: Check.

Our sanity: Unchecked!

As I waved at Tafesse from the hotel lobby, he quickly left his car to help us. We looked ridiculous, like a couple of clowns. Stuff dangled off every part of our bodies, with straps strafing our chests, others slapping against our thighs, while others oscillated back-and-forth between our biceps and forearms. Tafesse couldn't suppress laughter. As he helped untangle us, I thought, *Tafesse has seen all this count-less times before, I'm sure. Like all first-time parents, we brought everything we got from our baby showers, afraid that if we forgot something, our baby would die. Yep, we are* that *couple.*

As we left the hotel, Tafesse told us that the Gladney home was about twenty minutes across town. My stomach dropped. It felt like an eternity. It wasn't long before we found ourselves in the central artery of the city. I lost track of time immediately. The throb and pulse of Addis life was fascinating. One friend had told me that Addis felt like a dirtier version of New York City. This seemed fairly accu-rate. The air smelled like burnt tires and smog. There was an almost palpable haze that blanketed everything, including the steady stream of people who walked along the sidewalks. I noted the small shanties (locals call them *tuts*) that aligned the sidewalks with their corrugated tin roofs shining in the sun, and street vendors standing in the doorway, clucking their teeth and whistling at people to come in and check out everything from their fresh fruit to their fine linens.

Blue-colored taxis zipped by us. Most of these taxis were converted Volkswagen buses. Pointing them out to Tafesse, he told me that most Ethiopians walked everywhere, but sometimes, they would pay a couple birr (Ethiopian equiv-alent to dollars) to travel by taxi. Tafesse referred to these taxis as the "blue donkeys" because they were clunky, beaten up, and prone to mechanical problems. He promised I'd see herds of these taxis broken down on the side of the road. Not long after, I saw a blue taxi with a blown out front tire. It was hard not to suppress my laughter.

It wasn't long before Tafesse turned off the main highway and onto a dirt road. The ride got suddenly bumpier as Tafesse tried to avoid the potholes created by heavy rains and erosion. I didn't mind the shocks and jolts because I was too busy capturing the exotic swirl of activity with my camcorder.

The topography in the distance arrested my attention. I noticed a beautiful grove of eucalyptus trees growing out of a hillside. Their leaves were as long as elephant ears that hung heavy with lobbed fruit the size of footballs. Adjacent to the eucalyptus trees, I noted a small band of boys, no older than ten, snapping their whips and calling out in a chorus of strident voices for the herd of goats to move forward. Listening closely, I could hear the tramping hooves kicking up dust and their bleating noises mingling with the roar of car mufflers.

Moments later Tafesse stopped and parked the car outside a gated house. I had heard that the Gladney transition home was located in a new suburb. As I stepped out of the car, I could still see the house's fresh coat of paint glistening in the sun. Walking to the front door, I noted the long chicken wire that ran from the balcony to the front yard fence. Bright towels and baby outfits hung over the lines, some fluffy and snapping in the wind, others dangling limp, heavy with wetness.

Amy

Belay greeted Josh and me at the door and took us into a spacious living room, where tiny skeins of light filtered in through the windows. I could hear muffled baby cries seeping in through the ceiling floors. I had heard that there were as many as seventeen babies at the facility and just as many care workers. Listening closely, I could hear tiny feet shuffling from room to room, their movement brisk and fluid as they responded to the cacophony of cries. At that moment, I wondered which high-pitched scream might belong to Silas.

Once in the living room, I noticed that Margo and Clayton were already there, waiting with bottles and rattles in hand. Belay had already disappeared upstairs to find the Faulkners' little boy, Deacon. When Belay returned, Deacon was wide-eyed and alert, folding right into Margo's arms and laughing every time Clayton shook the frog-shaped rattle. I could feel the mascara smudging under my eyes. If ever there was a Hallmark moment, the Faulkners had one with Deacon. He was all gums and giggles. As Josh recorded most of their "gotcha" moment on the camcorder, I nervously shuffled back and forth like an alpine skier dangling her skies over the edge, waiting breathlessly to take the initial plunge.

Belay told us he would now go get Silas. We waited next to the window in a saucer of sunlight. I could feel the warmth on my back and the ripe smell of the deciduous banana plant next to us. Looking over at Josh, he was visibly twitchy, making a swizzle noise he inherited from his dad. My heart thumped around my chest like a tennis shoe in the dryer. My hands were shaking. I couldn't believe it was really happening. I had dreamed about it for months now, envisioning what I would feel the moment I saw Silas. Before I could register exactly what I felt, Belay turned the corner and appeared with our camcorder. The camera's lens burned a hole in my flushed cheeks. Suddenly a woman dressed in a white gown appeared. Her head was wrapped up in a scarf that reminded me of a baker's hat, and she was carrying my little boy, who was dressed in all pink right down to the pacifier. Silas's eyes were still heavy with sleep, and his eyelids flickered agitatedly as he tried to adjust to the diffused sunlight. The nurse's warm smile assured me that Silas wasn't like crystal china and that I wouldn't drop him. She must have felt my jitters. Gently passing Silas over to me, I quickly cradled him in my arms and pulled his frail little body up to my chest. In that moment, Silas felt like air, cotton, and bones in my arms. He was smaller in person than in his most recent pictures.

Josh tilted his head over my shoulder and introduced himself to Silas.

"Hey little fella, I'm your dad."

We both laughed and cried. Once Silas had fully adjusted to the light, his eyes dilated with terror, and before I knew it, he had spit out his pink pacifier and started screaming bloody murder. It wasn't long before he was gagging, heaving, and choking. Silas's eyes were like bulging disks, spinning madly with horror as though trying to escape from the filmy stare of Frankenstein's monster. Was I that hideous and scary looking? In that moment, I kind of understood what people must feel the moment before their lungs fill up with water and they drown. I turned to Josh and saw that he was treading water as frantically as I was. Swiveling my head in Belay's direction, I found the camera lens zooming in, capturing the kick and struggle of both of us. Trying to leaven the situation with humor, I exclaimed, "This wasn't how I pictured it," and everyone around us laughed, especially Margo and Clayton, who were still floating like astronauts in their own little solar system with baby Deacon.

In my mind's eye, I pictured our "gotcha" moment going a bit differently. I had hoped for a movie moment, where soft strains of music played in the background. As I looked into Silas's eyes and he stared back at me, our souls would touch. We would just know we were made for each other, and he would know with certainty that I would always be there for him, putting Band-Aids on his boo-boos, reading his favorite bedtime stories, praying for angels to protect him, and loving his future wife like my own daughter. I had the entire moment scripted out in my head.

I expected a fairy tale; what I got was a comedy.

Fortunately, the nurse wasn't finding the humor in my predicament. She picked up on my distress signal and quickly prepared a bottle of milk for Silas. Sitting down on the couch, I gave Silas the bottle, and after a while, the yummy goodness worked its way down to his stomach, causing his tense little body to relax and nestle into me. As I fed him, I could feel his rib cage pressed up against my chest, bony and sharp.

Eventually I handed Silas off to Josh. It was my turn to man the recorder. It was a funny scene as well. Josh held Silas like a running back holding a football, afraid to death he might fumble and lose the game. Silas's pink onesie and pink pacifier only added to the hilarity. It didn't matter, though. Within moments, Josh was in a different world, already seeing visions of bouncing a basketball and playing a game of Around the World out in the backyard with Silas.

After returning to our hotel, I couldn't wait to get Silas out of his pink outfit. I had four different onesies laid out on the bed.

I couldn't decide which one I liked best. I was like a little girl again in pigtails. Silas was my new Cabbage Patch Doll.

After unclothing Silas, I placed him on the bed. Silas rolled around naked, squealing with delight. He grooved like a hippie at Woodstock, free and unencumbered.

While Josh watched Silas, I went into the bathroom to draw Silas a warm bath. I was curious to see how Silas would react to water. I feared a shrieking outburst, like he had just seen the movie *Jaws*. I was pleasantly surprised. Silas splashed around like a happy fish. At one point, Silas slipped through my soapy hands and rolled over on his tummy. He had transformed into a surfer. Silas kicked his arms and legs like he was catching the barrel of a cresting wave. Josh and I cheered him on.

As our first day unfolded with Silas, I noticed little things, like Josh's love language with his new son. Regularly, Josh would lean down and give Silas a slobbery kiss. It sounded like a whoopee cushion. Josh called this kiss a "zerbert." With every zerbert, Silas's eyes would light up in Josh's smiling face, and Silas's eleven-pound body would spasm with laughter.

I also paid attention to my own small interactions with Silas. I found that I would break spontaneously into song anytime I held him. I vividly recall toweling Silas off from his bath, and as I did this, I sang him these lyrics:

I love my Silas
I love, I love my Silas
I love my Silas, myyy boooy!
I love my Silas
I love, I love my Silas
I love my Silas, my sweet little boy!

This song stuck. Every morning since, I have woken Silas up with this song. It's how we greet each other. It's my love song to my son. Moreover, it's a psalm of praise to my God for giving me a son to sing to each day.

As bedtime approached that first night with Silas, Josh and I played "rock, paper, scissors" to determine who got the first night shift. I lost. Honestly, I didn't mind. Soon after Josh had fallen asleep, Silas woke up hungry. I turned on the light, changed his diaper, and then turned the light off. The rest I did in the dark, by feeling. I took Silas into bed with me and propped myself up with pillows against the headboard to feed him his bottle. As Silas swallowed down the milk, he began a low contented sort of singing. I joined in, humming along under my breath. It was our first duet.

Looking back on that first day with Silas, it felt for a time like he was only present, enclosed mostly in his own small being. And then, I could see it happening, he began to look out of his eyes. He began to see the light from our hotel windows. He began to see us. He began to know us. He began to look at us and smile, as if greeting us from a world we did not know.

To know that I was becoming known by this small living being, who had existed 2,000 miles away but now was brought near to me through pain, desire, and love—that changed me. My heart, which seemed to have had only loss and grief in it before, now had joy in it. My heart was full. Through Silas I felt like I was setting out into a new world and into a new life.

I felt reborn.

Visiting Silas's Orphanage

Amy

The next morning we had the opportunity to visit a local orphanage. Silas had only stayed at the orphanage for a week before Gladney transported him over to their care facility. Still I was anxious to see firsthand what the conditions were like for orphans like Silas.

As we pulled up to the orphanage, Tafesse told us to prepare ourselves. The first time he had visited the facilities and seen the children, he had stayed in his car and wept. Stepping out of the car, I was immediately surrounded by children, ranging from the age of two to ten, many wearing the same turquoise-colored tops. Earlier, I had learned that the orphanage also served as an elementary school: half of the children were local kids, while the other half were orphans. It was easy to distinguish between them. The orphans wore tattered shirts, dirt-stained jeans, and holed-up shoes. When the children flashed me their beaming smiles, I noticed many with enflamed, licorice-colored gums and rotting teeth. Other children had noticeable skin abrasions on their arms and faces in webbed patterns. Looking over at Josh carrying Silas around in the Baby Bjorn, I suddenly felt something like shrapnel against my chest. I could see Silas in these children's faces. I could glimpse something of Silas's future in their eyes.

I could see Silas at ten years old, with holes in his jeans and lice in his hair.

I could see him at eighteen years old, with no education, no marketable skill, and no job prospects.

I could see Silas at twenty-two, phased out of the orphanage system, living on the streets, scrambling to survive, reduced to an animal like existence.

I could see him at twenty-five years old, either rotting in a prison cell for thievery or rotting in a grave due to a gang-related death.

Through such glimpses, I felt more fully the gravity of our decision to adopt Silas. I also felt sobered by the tragic consequences when we do not "defend the orphan" and do not take care of the "least of these."

From there, I was led into a nursery where the infants were kept. What immediately stood out was the lopsided ratio between children and workers. For every eight or nine infants, there was only one worker to meet their needs. I was saddened to think of how many of those children weren't getting the stimulation they needed to develop.[27] In addition, I was somewhat taken back by the heavy smells of urine, sweat, and dried feces that stung my nose and eyes. Looking down at my feet, I saw a dirty cot with ten infants almost stacked on each other, all swaddled in mangy blankets, some sleeping, others screaming. The nurse told me there was very little room left for the babies. It felt suddenly like I was in one of those commercials with children with bloated tummies and flies buzzing around their scabby faces, the kind that Sally Struthers hosts.

Leaving the nursery, I had to take a moment to collect myself. Suddenly I saw a flashing image of Silas sleeping on one of the dirty, uncovered cots, smelling of urine and sweat, flies buzzing around. I felt a wave of nausea come over me. I had to quickly blot out the thought and seek reprieve in the open air, where I found Josh. I recounted the lamentable details of the nursery, and he decided to refrain from personal experience—maybe a respectable attempt at blissful ignorance. I couldn't help but conclude, *This is not the way things were meant to be. This is not the world God created us for.*

Denim Boy

Josh

Not longer after Amy returned from visiting the infant room, a car pulled up carrying Rosemary, another Gladney adoptee. She had come to pick up her new eleven-year old son, Endie.

Earlier, I had noticed an older boy wearing a Nike baseball cap. He was sitting next to a boy garbed in all denim. They looked like two baseball catchers, crouched down, about to flash the pitcher a fastball sign. When Rosemary arrived and appeared from the back seat, the boy in the Nike cap sprang up like a grasshopper, sprinted over, and leaped into her arms. She laughed and twirled Endie's gangly body around in the air.

The boy clad in denim particularly captured my gaze. I was curious about his story. I deduced he was close friends with Endie, because wherever Endie went, denim boy followed like an afternoon shadow. Any time Rosemary asked the denim boy a question, he blanched and relocated his demure eyes.

The narrative mystery behind this reticent soul was heartbreaking. Both denim boy's parents had died when he was eight. For a couple years, denim boy lived with his grandmother. However, the grandmother was extremely poor and only able to feed denim boy one meal a day. When denim boy heard that the boys at the orphanage ate three square meals a day, he told his grandmother he wanted her to sign away her rights to him to the orphanage. Furthermore, denim boy had heard rumors from friends like Endie that he would get adopted by a nice family and get to go live in America. Come to find out, denim boy was one of the top students in his class (five out of sixty-five), and he had ambitions to go to medical school to become a doctor. Adoption would be his ticket to pursue this dream.

Now denim boy had to watch as his best friend left for the United States, and he had to stay behind to wait for a prospective adoptive family. Days later Rosemary described to us the heart-wrenching way denim boy clung to Endie, imploring him to stay or take him to America too. As Endie drove away, denim boy sprinted behind the car until the combination of the muffler smoke and sharp gravel stopped the boy in his tracks, leaving him only to wave, jump, and shout through the plumes of chalky dust as his best friend disappeared around the street corner.

As I watched denim boy's shadow grow long and then disappear into the eucalyptus trees, I looked down at Silas, who rested his head against my chest. I immediately reached down and kissed the top of his head. I looked up again hoping to catch one last glimpse of denim boy's lonely silhouette. He was gone.

A day hasn't gone by since where I don't think about denim boy. Often he appears to me in Silas's face. In those vexing moments, I can't help but wonder if our paths crossed for a reason. Perhaps I was meant to be denim boy's father. Maybe denim boy was meant to be Silas's bigger brother. These questions haunt me.

I also can't help wonder about the other 4.4 million children in Ethiopia, who, just like denim boy, daily feel their stomachs growl for food and daily feel their hearts ache for a family. When I wonder about this, I feel a deep pang inside, and I long for more families in America to come over, visit the orphanages, cradle babies like Silas, meet orphans like denim boy, look into their eyes, hug their bodies, and discover that these children are not statistics but God's special creations. Just like us, they are searching, questing, and hungering for a place of belonging.

God's Dreams

Josh

On Saturday night I received a call from a man named Berhanu. I had expected Berhanu to call us. Amy's blog friend from Washington, D.C., Anne, had told her about Berhanu and the church he pastored in Addis. Anne and Mike's church in Washington, D.C., supported Berhanu and his church.

After saying hello, Berhanu introduced himself and asked if we still wanted to visit his church in the morning. I told him yes, and if it was okay, Margo and Clayton wanted to join us. Berhanu was thrilled.

The next morning, Berhanu met the four of us in the parking lot outside a two-story concrete building. After greeting us, we climbed two flights of stairs that led into a small library. There were thirty chairs lined up neatly in five rows, separated by a narrow aisle. The room had that musty old book smell, which I loved as an English teacher.

Soon after I sat down, I heard the clacking sound of heels behind us, as a pack of women entered the library, frocked in ornate Sunday dresses, many with long colorful scarves flowing down to the middle of their backs. As they filed into the aisles, the women gave off an aura of restrained dignity that reminded me of pictures I had seen of Maya Angelou.

Behind the women a group of men scuffled in, wearing black and grey suits. The younger men sported hats that reminded me of Chicago gangsters in the 1920s. Both the men and women saw us and introduced themselves. Many asked if they could hold Silas and Deacon, kissing their tiny feet and stroking their faces.

The worship service started with Berhanu greeting everyone and then leading us in a hymn. As the room broke out into an a cappella chorus, I scanned the room, curious about the cross section of people. I had never worshipped with a black congregation. Suddenly, I felt a knifing pang of guilt when I was reminded of the truism: the most segregated hour in America occurs at 11 AM, when everyone is at church. I thought of all the churches congregating in the United States and how many of those churches were still divided along the color line. I felt crestfallen as I cradled Silas in my arms. Glancing over at Amy, though, I could tell that she was elated to be here. She swayed back and forth as she sang softly with those around her. She had never looked more radiant and incandescent.

I caught a glimpse of a young man seated one row behind us. He looked about twenty years old. As he sang, his scraggly dreads banged in the air like Jimi Hendrix. At the same time, I could hear a rich hum coming from behind me. I turned around and made eye contact with an elderly woman. She smiled as she broke into the song's chorus. Turning back around, I closed my eyes and allowed the deep cadence of her voice to pass through my soul like an African drum in the night.

At one point, Amy looked over at me and started laughing. I had loosened up a bit and was now bobbing and jamming like my dreadlock friend behind me. My whiteness, however, and lack of rhythm offered a humorous contrast against a sea of such black fluidity.

After we finished singing, Berhanu introduced Pierre, our speaker. Pierre had been living in Addis for two years, but he was moving to another country to take a new position with his company. Pierre reminded me of Sidney Poitier, with his dark skin, sharp jaw line, and penetrating eyes. Because this was Pierre's last Sunday, Berhanu had asked him to give a farewell sermon.

Pierre's message was on God's dreams. His main passage was from the Gospel of Matthew. Putting on his reading glasses, Pierre leaned over his Bible and read in a thick African accent:

> Because you have so little faith. I tell you the truth, if you have faith as small as a mustard seed, you can say to these mountains, Move from here to there and it will move. Nothing is impossible for you.
>
> Matthew 17:20

For the next twenty minutes, Pierre unpacked the meaning

of Jesus' agricultural metaphor. Pierre proclaimed that God had planted dreams in the soil of our hearts. These dreams were seeds. For some of us the seed was God's dream for peace. For others of us the seed was God's dream for justice. For another, equality. And for another, mercy. I'll admit it was nice to hear a sermon on dreams that didn't smack of the Americanization of the Gospel, specifically, the prosperity message of health, wealth, and power, not to mention fame.

After a while, Pierre worked up quite a lather, regularly having to pull out his handkerchief to wipe away the sweat beads from his forehead. Halfway through his sermon, Pierre did something quite unexpected. He pointed at us and exclaimed, "Just look at this couple here. God has given them a dream, and look how God is fulfilling it now." Then Pierre chuckled and pointed to my feet that wiggled through the straps of my Chacos. "Just look at this guy. He wears sandals, and yet look how God has used him."

Everyone in the aisles around me started laughing and shaking their heads. I chuckled, though I didn't know what was so funny. After the service, I asked Berhanu what the joke had been, and Berhanu slapped me on the shoulder and explained that in Ethiopia, if someone wears sandals to church, it means that they are "very, very poor."

Before Pierre ended his sermon, he came back around to us. Pierre had spoken directly to other individual members throughout the sermon. I could tell he took great pride in working loosely from his sermon notes. Pierre's word to us was that God had not only given us the dream of a child, but he had also given us a dream to work within the "fields of the fatherless." Something in that phrase hit a deep chord in me. Looking next to me, I saw Amy quietly crying as she stroked Silas's sleeping face. Pierre's word had struck a nerve with her too.

Personally, Pierre's word had invoked a memory in me from many years ago. While Amy and I attended a leadership meeting at our church, a visiting pastor from Kansas City asked if he might pray for us. Before the pastor did, however, he asked us a question: "Do either of you have a past working with underprivileged kids?" I surveyed Amy's eyes. We did. Amy had worked with youth in Dublin at a summer camp. I had worked three years as a counselor at Kannakuk's inner city camp, KAA (Kids Across America). Nodding to the pastor, he went on to share a word picture he felt he had received from the Lord. "In my mind's eye, I see both of you playing with many children in a poorer part of the world. I'm not sure if you are working at a camp of some kind or not, but nevertheless, I just sense that God has put in both of your hearts a desire to minister the Father's love to the fatherless."

Much later I was reminded of what Scott had told Amy and me during our first counseling session. "It sounds like both of you have clashing dreams." Scott's insight had cut to the root of our conflicts. What I didn't understand then that I do now is that what Amy and I really didn't have was a *common vocation*. Furthermore, I think clashing dreams happen quite often, especially in marriage, when the dreams we have are our own dreams, bathed in total selfishness rather than God's dreams for us. In my life, it seems his dreams continually counter mine. But as I allow God to implant his dreams in me, and likewise with Amy, our dreams converge.

I was reminded of another passage in Matthew where when Jesus had seen the crowds, he had compassion on them, and he said to his disciples, "The harvest is plentiful but the workers are few. Ask the Lord of the harvest, therefore, to send out workers into his harvest field" (Matthew 9: 37–38).

In the end, Pierre's word helped solidify the sense that Amy and I were called to the "fields of the fatherless" and that this was the place where our hearts' deepest longing and the world's deepest need were meant to converge in us for the rest of our lives.

Today, Amy and I continue to discover what our common vocation looks like in our daily life. Unequivocally, though, we sense we have heard the voice of the one who has summoned us to a common *mission*, with a common *task*, with a common *goal*, rooted and grounded in a common *dream*.

Meeting Hermela

Amy

One bit of exciting news we had received before we traveled to Ethiopia was that Josh and I would get to meet Tesfamariam's birth mother. In our referral packet, we had learned the names of both Tesfamariam's mother and father, and we were given a little bit of background information on both of them. As a result, Josh and I were eager not only to put a face with the name but also to learn as much as we could about Tesfamariam's heritage.

We met Hermela and her maternal grandmother at the Gladney facility the day before we left for home. Driving over, I felt jittery and nervous. I didn't know what to expect or how I would feel. I especially feared snagging my foot on an invisible trip wire in terms of what was appropriate questioning and what wasn't. I deeply wanted to cull as much as I could about Tesfamariam's family. I knew that one day

Tesfamariam would ask me about his family, and I wanted to inform him and honor his roots as best I could. At the same time, I wanted to respect Hermela's privacy. No doubt I felt a slippery slope underneath my feet.

When we arrived, Belay escorted us into the living room. Hermela and her grandmother were seated quietly on the couch. They stood and bowed to us. Suddenly I felt as if I were the quaking walls of Hoover dam, holding back an imminent flood.

Hermela was tiny and innocent looking. If I would have guessed her age, I would have placed her around my niece Kayla's age, at thirteen. She had similar features to Tesfamariam, a small nose, copper-colored eyes the size of pennies, and a high forehead. I noted that Hermela had unusually sable skin that looked like she had spent a lot of time under a canopy of intense tropical sun. Hermela's grandmother, however, was light skinned, like cinnamon. Her broad shoulders were covered in a shell-colored shawl, and noticeably, every time she spoke, her arms would flap, causing the shawl to grow and expand like the wings of a mother hen.

Initially, I could tell Hermela was terribly uncomfortable and uncertain as to whether she should ask to hold Tesfamariam or just sit back down next to her grandmother. With a gentle nod from her grandmother, however, Hermela tentatively reached out and cradled Tesfamariam into her arms. Tesfamariam was sleeping, sucking gently on his pacifier. I stepped back to give Hermela her space and time. I had fully prepared myself for Hermela to hold Tesfamariam the whole time we were together. I was surprised, then, when after only a handful of seconds, she returned Tesfamariam to my arms. Curiously, Hermela's face had been deadpan and expressionless the whole time. Shuffling back over to the couch, Hermela sat down and almost buried herself in her grandmother's shawl. I could tell that a part of Hermela wanted to disappear. Part of me felt the same way.

Sensing the awkwardness, Belay chimed in and told us that while we talked, one of the Gladney staff, a young Ethiopian woman, was going to perform the traditional coffee ceremony. For a while we sat in silence as the aroma of the roasted coffee beans wafted the air and watered our tongues with anticipation.

After a while, Hermela's grandmother broke the silence. She asked us if we had enjoyed our time in Addis Ababa. Belay sat near us and translated. I told her I had loved my time in the city and couldn't wait to return again some day. The grandmother then switched to more important questions, like whether we were religious and attended a church. She was Orthodox Christian. I told her we too were Christians, Protestants, in fact, and very involved in our church. She smiled at this and nodded her head. Then the grandmother turned her benevolent gaze upon Josh and asked him what he did for a profession. Josh politely explained his position as a teacher and coach. The grandmother smiled at Hermela and then said to him, "Both of us had hoped that Tesfamariam would be adopted by either an artist or teacher. This makes us very happy."

As we talked, I watched Hermela closely and noticed subtle spasms of curiosity, where her eyes would dart furtively in my direction then shift directions in a nanosecond to elude my eyes. She was like a thief trying to steal a peek at

Tesfamariam while leaving no trace of evidence. I ascertained that she tacitly ached to hold her child more, so I offered again. The grandmother quickly intervened, "Oh, no, no, we don't need to hold Tesfamariam anymore. We got plenty of chances to do that. Now it's your turn." Pulling up her shawl, the grandmother continued, "And don't you worry, one day Hermela will get married and have many more babies. In fact, when she does get married, we will send you an invitation." The grandmother chuckled to herself. I glanced over at Josh out of the corner of my eye. Was the grandmother joking or being serious? "Of course, you won't be able to tell anyone who you are, especially the groom," the grandmother quickly added. She was serious. I smiled and told her we'd be honored to receive an invitation.

Glancing over at Hermela, I felt like her posture was a veritable window into her fragile state of mind. At one moment, Hermela reminded me of the girl in Norman Rockwell's painting, "Girl at Mirror," sitting rigid and stiff, her arms and hands tentative and folded into her body like tendrils of a closed flower. Like the girl alone in the attic, Hermela looked like she was still living in that tenuous space between bud and blossom, between her teddy bear and lip stick, and between the world of make believe and the world of harsh reality. In that moment, a big part of me wanted to reach out and hug her. I wanted her to know how much God loved her and I loved her, that I felt her fears inside my chest, that I too was scared.

After some time passed, we found a nice flow to our conversation. We talked and listened, sipping black coffee and watching Tesfamariam sleep. Once in a while, we stumbled our way upon a topic that provided us both equal delights. Perhaps the funniest moment occurred when Josh asked Hermela whether Tesfamariam's biological father was tall or short. Standing up and raising and lowering his hand, Josh asked Hermela if the father was "this tall," as in six feet two inches, or "this tall," as in five feet three inches. Hermela giggled and pointed to the latter. Josh winced a bit and then exclaimed, "So he'll be a point guard!"

After we finished our coffee, Belay told us it was time for us to go. As I stood up to leave, Hermela got out a pencil, wrote down her address on a small piece of paper, and then handed it to me. After this, we all went out to the front lawn to take pictures. Josh and I towered over Hermela, who stood between us holding Tesfamariam. In most of the pictures, Hermela maintained a blank expression.

After a smattering of pictures, the grandmother and Hermela gathered together with Tesfamariam to say good-bye. I stood near the car to afford them ample space. Beneath my veil of tears, I could barely see the final exchange. What I do remember seeing was the grandmother kiss Tesfamariam's feet and then Hermela lean down, brush her cheek against her child's cheek, and kiss him softly on the forehead.

Neither Josh nor I spoke for the duration of the ride back to the hotel. I, for one, had sunk down into myself. In only a week, I felt like my heart had bonded so tightly to Tesfamariam that the thought of giving him up was unbearable. I couldn't have imagined what Hermela had felt when she handed Tesfamariam over to the orphanage, nor could I imagine what she felt now as we drove away, perhaps never to see her son again. Putting myself in Hermela's shoes, I

could understand why she had to distance herself emotionally from Tesfamariam. Who wouldn't have to resort to complete numbness in order to survive such a painful ordeal?
I still feel a flood in my throat every time I think of saying goodbye to Hermela. I'm almost certain the entirety
of my feelings in that moment will remain forever ineffa-
ble. Ambivalence is perhaps the best word I can muster to
describe how I felt. Part of me felt the *rightness* of adoption,
the *rightness* of God fulfilling a dream of ours, the *rightness*
of God meeting a need of Hermela's, and the *rightness* of
Hermela's courage and sacrifice. The other part of me felt
the *wrongness* of adoption, the *wrongness* of broken families,
and the *wrongness* of abject poverty. Reflecting back on the
times I had complained about my struggles with infertility
or I had expressed anger toward God for my life's unfairness,
I now felt remorseful and ashamed for what I had thought
and felt, how it all paled in comparison to Hermela's plight,
along with the hundreds of thousands of others like Hermela
who struggled every day just to survive.

In an ideal world, Hermela would never have had to give
up her child for adoption—for whatever reasons. Moreover,
in a world put back to rights, Ethiopia would never have to
open her borders again to outsiders like me to come in and
adopt their children. Instead orphanages would be filled with
empty beds, and adoption organizations would shut down.
In an ideal world, infertility would be nothing more than
a footnote in the annals of medical history. I guess, then,
partly what I felt as Hermela and her grandmother faded
in the distance through the rear view mirror was what Paul
felt when he wrote, "We know the whole creation has been

groaning as in the pains of child birth right up to the present time," (Romans 8:22) meaning that all of us on some level feel the wrongness of the world in our core. And maybe what that means is that until people like Hermela don't have to give up their children to infertile couples like us, none of us are meant to feel at peace in our skin.

As Josh and I talked about to whom we wanted to dedicate this book, we both immediately agreed. There would have been no story without Tesfamariam. And there would have been no Tesfamariam without Hermela's courageous choice.

So Hermela, wherever you are, I send out a prayer for you and thank the Father for your loving sacrifice.

A Father-Son Moment

Josh

After our time with Hermela and her grandmother, we went to the U.S. Embassy to pick up Silas' official paperwork. I thought the procedure would be painful, with a long wait, a grueling interview, and lots of signatures. Instead, the procedure lasted five minutes.

Leaving the embassy, I pulled out Silas' visa and passport and immediately noticed that his name had changed. The bold print read: Tesfamariam Josh. I asked Tafesse, our driver, if there had been some kind of misprint or mistake. Tafesse grinned and explained, "In Ethiopia, a child's last name is his father's first name. It's our tradition." I looked over at Amy in confusion. "So my name would be Josh Roc," I asked Tafesse, "and Amy's would be Amy Glen?" Tafesse nodded and said, "In our culture, naming one's child is a sacred act. It's a blood ritual. It denotes a very special bond."

That night, I woke up around 4:30 AM to Silas' whimper. Since it was my turn to take the night shift, I gathered Silas up in my arms and took him out onto the hotel patio, the only "cry proof" place in the hotel.

As I scanned my eyes across the city streets hushed under a blanket of fog and mist, I rocked Silas in my arms and sang quietly over him. Suddenly, an image surfaced and bobbed on the wake of my mind. It was of a photograph of my father and I, now yellow and faded with time. In the photo, I was scrunched up close to my dad like a koala bear. I must have been no older than Silas. Dad and I were at the beach, both wearing lemon-colored swim shorts. The sun reflected against our pale white thighs, and because of the sunhat on my tiny head, it was hard to see my freckled face or any of the tufts of my reddish-blond hair. Dad's face unforgettably was contorting and howling like a wolf as ten pounds of squirmy flesh scratched up against his chest hairs, sending tickle bumps through his body.

Dad looked young in the photo, younger than the current me, perhaps in his mid-twenties. He was already balding, although his years in the Air Force compensated: his body was sculpted like the ivory statue of a Greek Olympian. Notably, from Dad's posture, the Pacific winds must have been whipping up around him, because his right shoulder tilted slightly away from the ocean, protecting me from the spray of the surf and flying sand pebbles.

On the back of the photograph, my mom had written out

a short caption. The words were now hard to decipher. 1976. *Josh and Roc. Josh's 1ˢᵗ trip to the ocean.*

Silas suddenly interrupted my nostalgic thoughts. Staring up at me with mist and sleep gathered in his eyes, I rubbed the back of his head, which bobbled a bit in my palms. A sudden draft of mountain air whipped against my body. I felt goose bumps on the parts of my body that were exposed. I suddenly realized that all I was wearing were my boxer briefs.

Silas, however, was tucked under layers of blankets, and as I smiled and kissed his cheek, pulling him closer to my body, it suddenly began to settle in on me: Thirty years ago, I was my father's son. That day, I was Silas' father.

As the sun began to form like a ribbon on the mountain's ridges, I realized many things. I realized that I was in it for the long haul now. There would be a rash of midnight feedings, along with skinned elbows, broken bones, raging puberty, growing pains, natural curiosity, appetite-losing crushes, appetite-losing breakups, thrills of victory, agonies of defeat, doubts and questions, dreams and fears, and longings. For a moment, this protracted list caused my blood to freeze. I suddenly wondered if I would be for Silas half of what my father was for me. I wondered if I would fail Silas more often than I would succeed him. I wondered if Silas would ever come to spite me and want his "real father." But then, strangely, Tafesse's words returned to me about the sacredness of naming a son after the father. It suddenly resonated within me: from this point on, Silas' life and my life would forever be intertwined, like branches to a tree that shared the same plot of soil and the same ball of roots.

During the adoption period, I had secretly wondered if

the reality of being a father of an adopted child would feel like weight and if I would break under the pressure of it all. Surprisingly, I felt the opposite. In that moment, with Silas in my arms, I was air, light, and wind.

For the next hour, I walked around the hotel patio in circles. In the other room, Amy slept soundly. After a while, Silas fell back to sleep, and as Silas' little heart softly pattered against my chest, I felt the heartspace between my rib cages suddenly expanding, growing, and crackling as I realized what Tafesse had pronounced in the car: Silas was more than just my "adopted son."

From this day forward,

Silas was my *name*.

He was my *family*.

He was my *blood*.

And that would never change.

Epilogue

Amy

Silas and I have a bedtime ritual. He gets a bath, a bottle, and his favorite book, *8 Silly Monkeys*. Afterward, I hand Silas his velvety blanket, and he quickly scootches up to my chest and cuddles into me, clutching his blanket close to his body, smelling in that moment of soap and sweetness and fabric softener.

Sometimes, while I rock Silas in the darkness, I will pray for his protection, the way my mother prayed for me as a baby girl. Other times, I will just listen to the sound of his breathing against my chest. There are times, though, when I will recall moments from my journey to Ethiopia, and I will think to myself that Silas could have so easily grown up to become like the street children who approached our car, barefoot and ragged, their eyes hollowed with hunger, their hands cracked and callous as they begged for loose change. When I think about that, along with meeting Hermela and seeing many of the children at the orphanage, and I think about how my adoption journey with Josh has changed everything from my marriage to my family, from my faith to my dreams, I quietly realize this truth: *maybe all along, I needed Silas more than Silas needed me.*

A Final Note

Thanks for joining us on our journey from disorientation to adoption to transformation. If you have any thoughts or words you would like to share, or if you would like us to speak at your church, group, or organization, please contact us at:

www.fromashestoafrica.com

Endnotes

1. Leonore Fleicsher, *Shadowlands* (New York: Signet, 1993), 189. I would like to personally thank my twelfth-grade English teacher, Miss Faulkner, for giving me this book as my graduation gift. You were right, Miss Faulkner: the pain then was worth the happiness now.

2. T.S. Elliott, "Four Quartets," in *The Dry Salvages* (Chicago: University of Chicago Press, 1989).

Ashes

3. Frederick Buechner, *The Clown in the Belfry* (San Francisco: HarperSanFrancisco, 1992), 120.

4. Åshli O' Connell, "Childless couples grapple with emotional roller coaster, faith challenges," *Today's Pentecostal Evangel,* February 8, 2004, http://pentecostalevangel. ag.org/News2004/4683_childless.cfm.

5. William Shakespeare, *Much Ado About Nothing, a*ct 5, sc. 4.

I remember these lines only because I taught *Much Ado* for two years to my seventh-grade English students.

6. C.S. Lewis, *The Quotable Lewis* (Wheaton: Tyndale House, 1998), 250.

7. Annie Dillard, *Teaching Stones to Talk* (New York: Harper-Collins, 1983), 121.

8. "The Story of Emmy," *Invisible Children*, 2007, http://invisiblechildren.com.

9. Ken Gire, *The Reflective Life* (Colorado Springs: Chariot Victor, 1998), 67.

10. Richard Foster, *Prayer* (San Francisco: HarperSanFransico, 193), 55–56. I memorized these prayers from Richard Foster's chapter entitled "The Prayer of Relinquishment."

11. Brian McClaren, *A Generous Orthodoxy* (Grand Rapids: Zondervan, 2005), 110. McClaren references Leslie Newbigin, a contemporary theologian, who argues "that the great heresy (false, destructive, divisive belief) in monotheism results from taking the first half of God's call to Abraham (I will bless you, I will make your name and nation great) and neglecting or rejecting the second half (I will make you a blessing, all nations will be blessed through you)."

12. Amy Bottomly, *Ethiopia or Bust*, comment posted on September 11, 2007, http://www.bottomlysandetheopia.blogspot.com.

13. Buechner, *The Clown in the Belfry*, 77.

14. Frederick Buechner, *Wishful Thinking* (San Francisco: HarperSanFrancisco, 1999), 89. I can't tell you how many times I have returned to this lexical work to find a fresh articulation of shopworn Christian words and ideas.

Africa

15. Jody Landers, *The Lander's Adoption Blog*, comment posted on March 6, 2008, http://www.landersadoption.blogspot.com.

16. Tim Bascom, *Chameleon Days: An American Boyhood in Ethiopia* (New York: Houghton Mifflin Company, 2006).

17. Melissa Fay Greene, *There is No Me Without You* (New York: Holtzbrinck, 2006), 23–24.

18. Ronald J. Sider, *Rich Christians in An Age of Hunger* (Nashville: Thomas Nelson, 2005), 123. No book for us has been more theologically informative on themes related to the poor.

19. Nicholas D. Kristof, "Evangelicals a Liberal Can Love," *The New York Times*, February 3, 2008.

20. Tom Davis, *Red Letters: Living a Faith that Bleeds* (Colorado Springs: Cook, 2007), 79. I first saw Bono's speech on YouTube on March 21, 2007. Later I found the text verbatim in Davis's book.

21. John F. Alexander, "The Bible and the Other Side," *The Other Side*, no. 5 (1975). Alexander writes: "The fatherless, widows, and foreigners each have about forty verses that command justice for them. God wants to make it very clear that in a special sense he is the protector of these weak ones. Strangers are to be treated nearly the same as Jews, and woe to people who take advantage of orphans and widows."

22. Ken Gire, *The North Face of God* (Wheaton: Tyndale House, 2005), 23.

23. Shane Claireborne, *Irresistible Revolution* (Grand Rapids: Zondervan, 2007), 187.

24. Sider, *Rich Christians in an Age of Hunger*, 12.

25. Jim Wallis, *God's Politics: Why the Right Gets It Wrong and the Left Just Doesn't Get It* (San Francisco: HarperOne, 2006).

26. Eugene Peterson, *The Message* (Colorado Springs: NavPress, 1999).

27. Ibid. Sider writes: "Eighty percent of total brain development takes place between conception and age two."

Bibliography

Bascom, Tim. *Chameleon Days: An American Boyhood in Ethiopia*. New York: Houghton Mifflin Company, 2006.

Buechner, Frederick. *The Clown in the Belfry: Writings on Faith and Fiction*. New York: HarperCollins, 1992.

Buechner, Frederick. *Wishful Thinking: A Seeker's ABC*. Revised and Expanded Edition New York: HarperCollins, 1993.

Claireborne, Shane. *Irresistible Revolution*. Grand Rapids: Zondervan, 2007.

Davis, Tom. *Red Letters: Living a Faith that Bleeds*. Colorado Springs: Cook, 2007.

Dillard, Annie. *Teaching Stones to Talk*. New York: Harper-Collins, 1983.

Elliott, T.S. "Four Quartets." *The Dry Salvages*. Chicago: University of Chicago Press, 1989.

Fleischer, Leonore. *Shadowlands*. New York: Signet, 1993.

Foster, Richard. *Prayer: Finding the Heart's True Home*. 10th Anniversary Edition. San Francisco: HarperSanFrancisco, 1992.

Gire, Ken. *The North Face of God*. Wheaton: Tyndale House, 2005.

Gire, Ken. *Reflections on Your Life Journal: Discerning God's Voice in the Everyday Moments of Life*. Colorado Springs: Chariot Victor, 1998.

Greene, Faye Melissa. *There is No Me Without You*. New York: Holtzbrinck, 2006.

Kristof, Nicholas D. "Evangelicals a Liberal Can Love." *The New York Times*, February 3 2008. http://www.nytimes.com.

Lewis, C.S. *The Quotable Lewis*. Wheaton: Tyndale Press, 1998.

McClaren, Brian. *A Generous Orthodoxy*. Grand Rapids: Zondervan, 2004.

O' Connell, Ashli. "Childless couples grapple with emotional roller coaster, faith Challenges." *Today's Pentecostal Evan-*

gel, February 8, 2004, http://pentecostalevangel.ag.org/News2004/4683_childless.cfm.

Peterson, Eugene. *The Message.* Colorado Springs: NavPress, 1999.

Shakespeare, William. *Much Ado About Nothing.* New York: Washington Square Press, 1995.

Sider, Ronald J. *Rich Christians in an Age of Hunger.* Nashville: Thomas Nelson, 2005.

"The Story of Emmy." *Invisible Children*, 2007. http://invisiblechildren.com

Wallis, Jim. *God's Politics: Why the Right Gets It Wrong and the Left Just Doesn't Get It.* New York: HarperCollins, 2005.

Making a Difference in Ethiopia:

- Partnering to bring orphan care to Ethiopia

- Fighting the impact of HIV

- Connecting families adopting from Ethiopia

t Connected!!!

Living Faith to End Poverty

The Red Letters Campaign believes that **YOU** have the power to reduce extreme poverty, fight preventable disease and connect orphans with loving families.

We're a community that equips you and connects you with a network of partners and like-minded people to enable you to be an active part of the solution - the way you want to participate.

WWW.REDLETTERSCAMPAIGN.COM

"Sometimes I'd like to ask God why He allows poverty, famine and injustice in the world when He could do something about it...but I'm afraid God might ask me the same question." ~Anonymous

Join Tom in the fields of the fatherless. Turn what you've read into action by being Christ's hands and feet through many opportunities with Children's HopeChest, a leader in international orphan care.

GET CONNECTED

ENCOUNTER the living Christ in the fields of the fatherless. Join us on a vision trip. Call us for more information about our next vision trip to Africa or Eastern Europe.

JOIN the 5 for 50 Campaign. Children's HopeChest is proud to participate in the 5 for 50 campaign—5 practical ways to make a positive impact in the lives of nearly 50 million people suffering from AIDS worldwide. Go to **www.5for50.com** and make your pledge to help orphans in Africa. You can make a difference for as little as $5/month.

VISIT www.hopechest.org to find out more about how you can care for orphans through the programs of Children's HopeChest.

CONNECT OTHERS

INVITE your pastor. We believe in this so much that we offer pastoral scholarships as an investment in your church's ministry to orphans. Call the outreach team at Children's HopeChest.

STAY CONNECTED

READ Tom Davis' Blog. Tom regularly visits Russia, Africa, and other places around the globe. He updates his blog regularly with videos and reflections on his experiences, and shares current information on orphan care. **www.cthomasdavis.com**

DRINK Saint's Coffee. With every pound of this fair trade and organic coffee purchased, you will feed an orphan for a month.
www.saintscoffee.com

800.648.9575 • www.hopechest.org

CHILDREN'S HOPECHEST
Confidence to fly and a safe place to land

100% of net profits are reinvested in the lives of orphan children.

Gobena Coffee offers fresh-roasted gourmet fair trade, organic, shade-grown coffee delivered right to your door. We are committed to offering the finest quality coffees from regions around the world. Each coffee is skillfully roasted in small batches for peak quality and freshness.

The Purpose:

In addition to experiencing the finest and freshest coffee, with each order placed, you are helping children throughout the world. **100%** of the profits are being reinvested in the lives of orphan children through charity programs.

To place your order, go to www.gobena.org